The Land That Is Very Far Off

Also by Dottie Mae Goard

These Last Days: Angelic Messengers Reveal the Future

The Land That Is Very Far Off

Dottie Mae Goard

Hope Publishing House, Pasadena, California

For information address:
Hope Publishing House
P.O. Box 60008
Pasadena, CA 91116 - U.S.A.
Tel: (626) 792-6123 / Fax: (626) 792-2121
E-mail: hopepub@loop.com
Web site: http://www.hope-pub.com
Cover design — Michael McClary/The Workshop

Printed in the U.S.A. on acid-free paper

Library of Congress Cataloging-in-Publication Data

Goard, Dottie Mae, 1925–
The land that is very far off / Dottie Mae Goard.
p. cm.
ISBN 0-932727-92-1
1. Goard, Dottie Mae, 1925– . 2. Christian biography– –United States. 3. Private revelations. 4. Second Advent. I. Title
BR1725.G56A3 1998
248.2'9– –dc21 97-38488
CIP

Dedication

This book is dedicated to my Lord and Savior Jesus Christ.

Acknowledgements

My sincere appreciation goes to all those who have reviewed the manuscript of this book and assisted in its preparation: Karin Hartline, Joyce Bond, Don and Thoral Haskell, Freda Marion and Della Craighead.

A special word of thanks goes to Faith Annette Sand, editor and publisher, for her skill in preparing the book for publication and for the kind and loving way she has dealt with me, and especially for her prayers.

I offer profound thanksgiving to my Lord and Savior Jesus Christ who guided me in the living of these experiences, who blessed me all along the way and who directed the writing of this book.

Table of Contents

Preface

The peace I experienced as I sat on the stone wall beside the Chapel of the Beatitudes in Northern Israel was a peace only the Lord can give. This was the spot, or somewhere nearby, where Jesus preached the Sermon on the Mount, which included the eight Beatitudes. Gazing across the meadow that sloped down to the beautiful blue Sea of Galilee, I thought about the crowds of people who had followed Jesus here and had sat quietly listening to the words of wisdom he spoke.

Mesmerized by the scene before me, I reflected on those Beatitudes: the blesseds our Lord draped upon the poor, the meek, the humble, the sad, the merciful, the pure. Nowhere did he offer a blessing for the rich, the powerful, the intelligent, the talented or the influential. The attributes admired by the world were not important to Christ.

An experience earlier that morning reinforced my determination to proceed with the writing of this book. A prayer meeting had been announced in this holy place for those of our tour group who wished to be prayed for. We were invited to step forward, and we all did.

When my turn came, Schlomo, a young Jewish scholar who

was a minister of the Gospel, laid his hands on my head, prayed for me and relayed a message from the Lord: "The Lord tells me you have walked with him for a long time," he said. I nodded as I reflected on this statement. "Also, he has given you the gift of song," he added, smiling. Continuing to quote the Lord, he appended, "You are to keep a journal of your religious experiences."

This young man could not have known that I have kept a journal of my encounters with God for many years and my first book, *These Last Days* (Hope Publishing House, Pasadena, CA, 1994), was based on the experiences recorded in those journals. Neither did he know that the book was filled with messages God had given me using songs and hymns. Yes, indeed, music was important to me and still is. I sing my way through every day.

Two of the three messages Schlomo gave me that day confirmed what I knew to be true, so it was comforting to verify that the messages came from God. The third message concerning my Christian walk gave me the spark needed to set me off on this new writing adventure.

Introduction

"Who among us shall dwell with devouring fire?
Who among us shall dwell with everlasting burnings?
He who walks righteously and speaks uprightly,
He who despises the gain of oppressions,
Who gestures with his hands, refusing bribes,
Who stops his ears from hearing of bloodshed,
And shuts his eyes from seeing evil:
He will dwell on high;
His place of defense will be the fortress of rocks;
Bread will be given him.
His water will be sure.
Your eyes will see the King in his beauty;
They will see the land that is very far off."
Isaiah 33:14b-17

Shortly after my first book *These Last Days* was published, the Lord God impressed upon me that I was to write another book. He had been continuing to send prophecies of the approaching close of the age when this world will wind down, when Jesus will return and judgment will come upon all people. The Isaiah prophecy, quoted above, gives us much sound advice and comfort as the "Day of the Lord" approaches.

This Scripture has always held great meaning for me, especially since I have taken seriously God's instruction to protect the entryway into my eyes, ears, mouth and spirit. Also he has impressed on me the necessity to guard my tongue from sin–using the carrot-and-stick method of teaching to get my attention. When I have sinned against him, he has withheld his Spirit from my consciousness, leaving me empty and alone. When I have been obedient in some sacrificial way, he has rewarded me with what a friend calls "warm fuzzies," and I have known I was on his team. Many times his rewards arrived as visions and verbal instructions concerning not only my affairs, but also global and cosmic circumstances.

And so now I feel impressed that God wants me to share my life, including these additional visions and prophecies, with the world. In the hope and assurance that people will grow in knowledge of God and what is required in their lives by reading about the things that have happened to me, I offer this book.

1

A Time of Change

A soft breeze belied the condition of my heart that spring morning. Though it had been more than a month since my husband Howard died, I was still grieving. The shock of seeing the person I loved and laughed with lying on the floor in the complete stillness of death left a deep furrow in my consciousness that may never be filled.

For what seemed like hours, but was really only eight minutes, I sat on the floor outside of the bathroom where he lay, waiting for the emergency team to arrive. But before it did, I either saw or felt a "whoosh" of spirit pass over my head. Later, I became convinced that spirit was an angel or a team of angels taking him to heaven.

The next few days were occupied with telephone calls, arrangements, receiving dozens of friends who came to visit and console, ordering a grave marker–and numbly staring out the window wondering what I was to do.

At the front of the house where Howard had tenderly planted a pink dogwood tree, beautiful full blooms appeared on every twig the same week he died. Its cross-shaped flowers were stained a delicate shade of pink, as though the Lord added a bouquet outside of the house to match the profusion of plants inside.

I do believe the Lord warned me this was coming. At least I attributed it to this when the Lord showed me Howard's face and inserted in my mind a comforting song, "In the Garden." This message arrived the day before he collapsed, but the Lord had been signaling me for at least two years that he was going to take Howard soon.

I actually think he told Howard, too, for one of his friends reported a comment Howard made the day before he died. After building shelves with a friend all afternoon, Howard turned to a bystander and said, "You'll have to help Warren finish these shelves," and then he walked out.

How can I adequately express my gratitude to my friend Miriam who never left my side for a full week. Miriam is a special, once-in-a-lifetime comrade. She is short of stature but solidly built, completely white-haired, full-bosomed and has permanent laugh lines in the corners of her eyes. Her keen sense of loyalty makes for enduring friendships, and in any challenging situation, she presents a courageous front for truth.

Miriam reported a message from the Lord to be given to me, saying, "I will give her proportionately according to her needs," and Miriam's daughter Deborah added, "His (Howard's) promise has been fulfilled, and she (Dottie) is blessed to have brought him to it. Now she will serve the Lord totally. She is very blessed." I felt the peace of God flowing through my body because of the prayers of friends and I was certain blessing would follow.

The morning after Howard's death our wonderful choir director Jerry Peterson showed up at my door. Besides being a musical genius, Jerry has a fabulous intellect. He is always working on some academic degree or other, though he already has a drawer full of them. Jerry's sensitivity to the spirit world is phenomenal. He has a strong inner awareness of heaven, having lost his first wife shortly after their marriage. Jerry had come to tell me something the Lord showed him.

In the night Jerry received a vision of what he thought was heaven. He saw a beautiful estate with green grass. On the grass stood a circle of chairs, one empty, but the rest of them filled with people. They were all talking about Howard. In the next moment, he saw Howard seated in the chair that had been empty, and on his face was a wide, sweet smile. When I think of him now, I see that smile.

I have relied on this as explicit proof that Howard is in heaven, and it has comforted me tremendously. Another gift from behind the veil also came from Miriam, who heard a message from the Lord as she was driving down the street. God said, "Howard is listening to Bach!"

How exciting! And what splendid news. We will actually see, hear and experience the great artists of the past, in person so to speak. Besides that, we will meet all of the old saints: Peter, Paul, Abraham, Moses, Elijah, Ruth and Esther, Hezekiah, Hannah, Daniel and all the other saints, both old and recent. *"And I say to you that many will come from east and west, and sit down with Abraham, Isaac, and Jacob in the kingdom of heaven"* (Mt 8:11). It reminds us to study the whole Bible now in order to know those we will meet in heaven.

I must not forget to relate the story Nancy told me a few days after the funeral. In my opinion Nancy knows God better than any of us in the morning prayer group, and I would trust her messages and visions from the Lord without any salt added.

She said she saw a band of light around Howard's head when he had stood to sing in the Sunday night worship service a few hours before he died. She thought it was a halo. I am also comforted to remember his being on his knees beside me at the altar rail at the close of that service.

God has been very near. Many nights I see the bright jewels of heaven or the fog bank of the Holy Spirit come into the room. Accompanying that is the complete, all-over embrace of the Spirit of God–a tingling and quivering of my whole body, along with the heat of the Holy Spirit. I also hear the far-off sounds of heaven as voices and songs: *The noise of a multitude in the mountains, like that of many people! The tumultuous noise of the kingdoms of nations gathered together* (Isa 13:4).

One morning I wakened to the sweet taste of honey in my mouth and I thought of the promised land of milk and honey that was given to the children of Israel. In my mind, it is like the land that is very far off–heaven.

I have prayed every night for God to post angels around the house, in the house, above it and below it for protection. I'm certain they are here for I have not been frightened at all and my dreams are sweet. Someone suggested that since I was now living alone, I should put in a security system. When I asked the Lord about it, he reminded me of the story of Elisha being protected by an army of angels when the king of Syria came after him. I became confident God would protect me in like manner.

The first week after Howard died I listened to the entire twelve tapes of the New Testament at night on the tape recorder. These great words were a healing balm to a grieving spirit.

A strange vision came to me a few nights later. I awakened in the middle of the night seeing the vision of a man's back. He was walking away from me. He had dark short hair; I could see

With such glorious visions, the Lord of the Universe continued to show me his love and care. One night I wakened, deep in the Spirit, heard the din of eternity and felt the embrace of the Holy Spirit, which renders one unable or unwilling to move. In the middle of the room, a whirlwind of light circled about a central spot. This faded, and on the wall sparkling jewels of every shade started flashing around in a circle. There were diamonds, amethysts, rubies, sapphires, emeralds, golden topaz and others I could not name. Slowly, I could make out a chair or throne as though drawn in dark and light lines within the center of the circle. The colored lights that were floating about the room gathered in a straight line of all the colors of the spectrum and formed a border above the throne.

This vision was similar to the one John relates in Revelation 4:2-3: *Immediately I was in the Spirit; and behold a throne set in heaven, and One sat on the throne. And he who sat there was like a jasper and a sardius stone in appearance; and there was a rainbow around the throne, in appearance like an emerald.*

A description of the heavenly jewels is found in Revelation 21:19-20: *And the foundations of the wall of the city were adorned with all kinds of precious stones: the first foundation was jasper, the second sapphire, the third chalcedony, the fourth emerald, the fifth sardonyx, the sixth sardius, the seventh chrysolite, the eighth beryl, the ninth topaz, the tenth chrysophrase, the eleventh jacinth, and the twelfth amethyst.*

As I watched in awe, the whole panorama drifted away. When it passed through the wall, the wall became transparent, and I continued to see the magnificent glory of God until it faded out into space. I was left feeling the heat of the Holy Spirit throughout my body for hours. How awesome is our Lord's care for us!

From these visions I knew the Father was opening up the portals of heaven to assure me Howard was safely with him. In addition, words of comfort started pouring in from friends all over the country.

Sometime later I received this letter from Washington state, written by a man who had been in the youth group we sponsored at our church years ago.

Dear Dottie,

I was deeply saddened to learn of Howard's untimely death earlier this year and wanted to write but did not have an address until now. How well I remember, and with such great fondness, the youth group meetings that you and Howard hosted in your home those many years ago. There was always classical music, intelligent discussions, warmth and love from the two of you that meant a lot to us as we were growing up. And of course, the memories of those times will last a lifetime.

Howard was a wonderful man with many fine qualities, and I know how close the two of you were. He will be sorely missed by those of us who had the good fortune to know him. As you may know, I lost my wife, Mary, last Christmas in an automobile accident. So I know from personal experience what it is like to lose a loved one.

You have my deepest sympathy in this time of great loss.

Sincerely, Adam B.

My answer to Adam quickly followed:

How pleased I was to receive your letter. It did bring back memories of that fine group of youth we worked and played with early in our marriage. Though I have looked back at times with embarrassment at how little of the faith we knew to teach, I am pleased that you received the love we had for you. Perhaps that sufficed.

Adam, my dear friend, I did not know of your loss. How tragic life is at times. I can imagine that you are still reeling from the blow and wondering how you can get life back together.

I had Howard 41 years, and though it is sometimes lonely around here, I can make it because I know where he is and that I will soon be joining him. God himself sent the comfort and assurance.

Adam, I know that at times you may wonder about the meaning of it all – why things happen as they do and why there is so much suffering on earth. I can't completely answer the question, but I do know some truths:

1. Suffering helps us to grow stronger in character and brings us closer to the Lord, if we seek God diligently.

2. There is eventual justice. Psalm 97:2b says "Righteousness and justice are the foundations of his throne."

3. No matter what happens, God does love us and has made plans for us to be with him forever – in this life and beyond this life.

4. The only thing of significance that we can take with us into the next dimension is love, so we must learn to love while here on this earth.

5. God has a plan for people to follow while in this life. If we follow his plan, love and joy and peace will come in spite of the circumstances. (Remember the Apostle Paul sat in a dungeon with his feet in stocks, his back beaten and bleeding, roaches and rats running across his body; he was cold, sick and hungry, but he also sang praises to God because he knew eventually all this pain would go away, and he would be with Jesus forever in the most beautiful place one can imagine.)

6. I know that my sins are forgiven because I have asked for that in the name of Jesus.

7. I know that one can actually sense the presence of God with every one of the five senses: sight, sound, smell, taste & touch. I have seen the blinding light of his presence in the dark of night; I have heard the ringing of joy-bells of heaven deep in my inner ear; I have smelled the exquisitely beautiful "odor of a sweet smell" spoken of by Paul, when God is near; I have tasted heavenly Communion; and I have felt the electric touch of the Holy Spirit on my lips when I have been commissioned to speak out for God in behalf of good over evil.

8. One can find no peace on earth without him because that is why we were made – to have fellowship with God and to live with him forever.

9. God's presence is more easily felt when we are praising him – either in words, actions or songs. Psalm 22:3 says

God inhabits the praises of people.

One very valuable tool I have learned to use during sleepless nights is listening to the Scriptures. I put in a Bible tape, turn it on and listen until I go to sleep. I listen every night when I get to bed, and if I waken in the middle of the night, I turn it on again. You might try it.

In the meantime, I offer you this great old Hebrew blessing, "May the Lord bless you and keep you; may the Lord make his face to shine upon you and be gracious to you; may the Lord lift up his countenance upon you and give you peace both now and evermore" (Num 6:24-26).

Love of Christ,

2

The Intruder

Even before Howard left to live with the Lord I was detecting something or someone in the house. When I would enter a room, I felt a spiritual presence. I saw movement out of the corner of my eye; I heard a rustling; I saw a leg in blue jeans disappear around the corner; I heard my name called by someone with a voice similar to Howard's, but Howard was in bed asleep at the time. I thought it might be an angel, but angels don't wear blue jeans. I *knew* it was not physical. It was also not evil; at least I felt no coldness. Job had this same experience: *"Then a spirit passed before my face; the hair on my body stood up. It stood still but I could not discern its appearance . . ."* (Job 4:15-16).

At first I thought some teenager was having an out-of-the-body experience in my house. Well, I reasoned, I can fix that. I anointed the house and ordered out anything not of the Lord. *But it didn't go!*

One night I awakened to see someone in blue jeans walking into my bedroom and up to my bed. The walk was like Howard's, but the body was the size of a teenager. At first I thought it was Howard coming to waken me for morning. I sat up in bed and opened my mouth to say, "Is it morning already?" when the *apparition vanished.*

I immediately walked through the house praying and again ordered out everything not of the Lord. When I went back to sleep, I suffered a screaming nightmare about a man in the house and Howard shook me awake. When morning finally arrived, the Holy Spirit touched me with the electric trembling I have come to know and love. When all of that stopped, I felt *two hands in the middle of my back!* It was the disembodied spirit back again!

Some weeks later, after Howard died, the spiritual presence made itself known in the house again. I finally told the whole wild tale to the morning prayer group, hoping they would not think I had completely lost my sanity. Immediately, Miriam started shaking and crying. She sobbed, "Dottie, the Lord says he is an intercessor."

Just then, I started shaking and crying, and we both said at the same time, "He is *my/your son!*" Years ago I lost a three-month pregnancy. We never knew the sex of the child, but I always thought it was a boy.

The next day was Sunday and I was sitting in the church congregation weeping a little, but also in prayer about having a teenaged son in heaven with Howard. Just then Wilson, the organist, started playing "From Heaven Above to Earth I Come," by J. Pachelbel. I was filled with thanksgiving to realize the spirit in my house was not an intruder, but *my son!* What wonderful news it was to know I had a half-grown son in heaven whom I will eventually see and know! I decided to start calling him James, since that name came to me immediately.

From the moment I knew who really was visiting me, the signs of the visitation stopped, and I never saw or felt him in the house again. But thanks be to God for showing him to me twice in visions. The first time, I wakened in the Spirit, looked at the ceiling and saw lumps of clouds forming. They looked muddy so I didn't know who was sending the vision. I called out, "Jesus, Jesus, praise him!" The clouds parted showing a roadway composed of red velvet trimmed on either side with gold braid in an intricate pattern and sprinkled with jewels of heaven. It was so beautiful I gasped.

That vision faded and at the side I saw two faces looking over a fence or barrier. One face was a man who looked like Howard and the other a boy whose face strongly resembled Howard's. This vision was in pencil sketch, so to speak, not living color. But the next time, I saw my son as though a color photograph closeup, and Howard's face was still looking over the fence to watch my reaction. Neither of them have I seen since then. I do not know why God gave me this special gift, but I am giving glory to him for this revelation.

Though I have not seen Howard since these visions of him with our son, one night at least two years after his death I heard him call my name in the middle of the night. I sprang awake instantly and looked around. Of course no one was there, but the voice itself was enough to bring tears to my eyes. It was a gentle, loving voice, a voice of caring and concern for me. I'm certain it came as a gift of assurance that he is happy and in heaven with the Lord. Perhaps the Lord allowed him to come and inspect the beautiful park I have created out of our vacant lot.

A year after Howard died, I was driving to Missouri to visit my sister, singing hymns and reciting memorized Psalms. I started thinking about Howard and wondering what goes on in heaven. Finally, I said to God, "Father, what is Howard *doing* up there?" No ready answer came so I put the question aside.

The next morning at breakfast my sister Betty said, "Dottie, I had a weird dream last night. I was playing with and petting large cats: lions and leopards and cheetahs." She grimaced and added, "I had my arms around their necks, petting them and playing with them. But I don't even *like* cats! Never have."

Then I started laughing and weeping at the same time. Here was my answer from God. Howard was petting and playing with large cats. He had always liked cats and often mentioned wanting a pet bobcat. God had answered my question by way of a dream to *my sister.* (And to those who often wonder if they will see their pets again in heaven, here is the answer: They certainly will.)

Heaven has been strongly on my mind since Howard moved there and since I know we have a son there with him. I actually received a vision of heaven or the New Jerusalem one night. I wakened in the Spirit to see a cube come down through the ceiling of the bedroom. It was about a foot cube, and it had many tiny layers of lights and jewels making it look like a model of the multi-storied cube described in Revelation 21:16 which is 1,500 miles in length, width and depth. Somehow it was communicated to me that this vision was symbolic of the New Jerusalem and was really very large. When it disappeared, I was left with the indwelling Spirit of God in my head as ringing bells and electricity. It almost felt as though I were being electrocuted. How awesome is our Lord!

A little later God sent on the ceiling of my bedroom a vision of stones fitted together across the entire ceiling, but the wonder of it was that between the stones shone a glistening white light, the most beautiful white I have ever seen, a silvery-white light. Though I love bright colors, I could be happy with that silvery-white light forever. No doubt God was showing me the underside of the pavement of heaven.

The Lord is making it clear to me in so many ways that my loved ones have gone to heaven and exist in a state of joy and ecstasy. A series of visions started one night when I was awakened in the Spirit and felt waves of electricity go through me. I heard in my inner being the hymn, "When the Saints Go Marching In," and saw a long line of spirits marching by my bed. They were foggy forms the size of people. One had a beautiful purple light around the head so I knew Jesus was participating in the parade.

After a while I slept, but early in the morning the Spirit wakened me and on the east wall appeared a ladder with foggy forms moving up and down. I laughed aloud at this vision of Jacob's ladder (Gen 28:12). The forms were angels ascending and descending from heaven to earth to bring comfort, instruction, protection, assistance and peace. Dear God, how I love you!

I am still puzzling over a giant head I saw in a vision. It was more wrinkled than anything I have ever seen and was completely without hair. Even the wrinkles had small wrinkles, and they had tiny wrinkles. The head was round; I seemed to be seeing it from the side and slightly above. I could see eyes placed normally, but there was an extra eye in the forehead, and I could see it very well. It was hazel colored, a light brown. I puzzled just who this could be. The next morning the Lord sent the hymn, "Praise the Lord, Ye Heavens Adore him," by Franz Joseph Haydn.

> *Praise the Lord! ye heavens adore him; Praise him angels, in the height; Sun and moon, rejoice before him; Praise him, all ye stars of light. Praise the Lord, for he has spoken; Worlds his mighty voice obeyed; Law which never shall be broken; For their guidance hath he made.*
>
> *Praise the Lord! for he is glorious; Never shall his promise*

fail; God hath made his saints victorious; Sin and death shall not prevail; Praise the God of our salvation! Hosts on high, his power proclaim; Heaven and earth and all creation laud and magnify his name.

Since then I have seen this hazel-colored eye many times. Sometimes at night I see it in the corner of the room or near the bed. I have seen it alongside many visions, not moving but sparkling like a living eye. I have been very puzzled concerning this vision. The whole matter called for Biblical search.

Several references in the Bible speak of God's *eye,* a *single eye:* Job 29:11; Psalm 32:8; Ezekiel 5:11; 7:4, 9; 8:18; 9:10. Psalm 33:18 says, *Behold, the eye of the Lord is on those who fear him, on those who hope in his mercy.* Besides that, there are many references to the plural *eyes* of God; for instance, in Psalm 34:15: *The eyes of the Lord are on the righteous, and his ears are open to their cry.* So both the *single eye* and *plural eyes* are attributed to God.

In addition, Ezekiel 10:12 states that the wheels of fire that represent the presence of God had eyes: "*... and the wheels that the four had, were full of eyes all around.*"

No one can see the face of God and live. *But [God] said, "You cannot see my face; for no one shall see me, and live"* (Ex 33:20). It is logical, therefore, that the very old head I saw was not God but the symbol of God, just as the wheel of fire carrying the four living creatures was a symbol of God (Ezek 10). Allowing my imagination full rein, I have thought that the two normally placed eyes on the ancient head might represent God the Father and God the Son, and the hazel-colored eye on the forehead might represent God the Holy Spirit. It could be a perfect symbol for the Trinity – three eyes working together for the same purpose, having the same will, operating on the same plan.

One night after I had witnessed to a small audience about

the prophecies in my first book and the many ways God had spoken to me and helped me, the Lord sent his Whirling Wheel into my bedroom. I wakened to see, not a vision on the wall, but *an object in the room*—a set of whirling wheels with fire on the inside of the box-like structure. A whirling wheel framed each side of the box! I was astonished! When the whirling wheels finally stopped I could see a living eye on the end of each spoke. The wheel had no rim. What a marvelous gift God gave me that night! I am continually amazed at his goodness. Praise God for his graciousness and love.

The interrelationship of the members of the Trinity was portrayed in a true story told to me by a friend. Christie was driving back from Tulsa behind her husband, who was bringing their newly repaired pickup truck home. She was occupied with worry about two boys, her son and his friend, whom they had left at home to clean up a vacant lot. She knew that no matter what they did, it wouldn't be done well enough for them to avoid a severe scolding by her hard-to-please husband. She continued to fret about it, then finally said to God, "You just don't know how I feel."

She momentarily side-stepped the worry and began to sing a praise song, when the booming voice of God said, "*I* don't know how you feel!" She was startled almost out of her wits, but managed to mumble something. Again the strong voice said with even more emphasis, "*I don't know how you feel!*"

"But this is my son, and he is so young and innocent," Christie said with concern.

"*My Son* was stretched out on a cross and crucified," the Creator of the Universe said, adding, "and he was innocent too."

With sympathy Christie said, "Oh, I couldn't have stood to watch."

"Neither could I," God said, and continued, "and he had

done nothing to deserve it." Then he added gently, "I turned my face away, and the whole world became dark." *Now when the sixth hour had come, there was darkness over the whole land until the ninth hour* (Mk 15:33). It appears that God the Father had withdrawn God the Holy Spirit from the earth while God the Son was being crucified.

3

Intercession

The Lord gave me the spiritual gift of tongues several years ago. During the weeks of mourning for Howard, God did not call upon me to use this spiritual praise to him. But the spirit prayer did return in force later, and one day in late spring my lips started trembling and twitching, characteristic of the call to prayer. Then God sent a patriotic song to my mind, and I knew the prayer should be for our nation. I did pray fervently both in English and in tongues.

That same night God sent a vision of two bandoliers crossed. On one bullet was the picture of an American flag plus a skull and crossbones. So the call to prayer may have been sent to protect the president and government officials against terrorists. I never knew the details of the attempted attack, only that everyone was safe. At that time I felt in my body the fatigue of those involved in the protection of our government officials.

Another incident of intercession on behalf of the nation

began with words that came one morning. As I awakened I distinctly heard the message, "Thank you for taking all necessary risk in behalf of the country." But it wasn't for me. The Lord sent the old World War I song "Over There" to let me know it had something to do with the president's mission to Russia just then, January 1993. The next morning a similar message came: "If we get the right agreement, we can hire our own guests." What could these messages mean? The only thing I could do was to pray for safety of our president and our nation.

Many times the morning prayer group has interceded for the sick who have been healed by the power of God through the Holy Spirit. Both physical and emotional problems have succumbed to that holy power.

Karen, a young mother, reported her twelve-year-old son had Tourette's Syndrome. He made noises with his mouth, hiccupped, blinked, coughed and stuttered at inappropriate times. He was not even in the room when we verbally cast out that affliction in the name of Jesus and by the power of God, and it left. The Lord sent a song with a line in it, "Born to set my people free," to let us know he had freed Allen from the tic. The problem returned a few months later, but Karen herself cast it out and it vanished.

We have used the same method of prayer with many people afflicted with infirmities and diseases. Lumps have disappeared from the bodies of two teenagers and one adult man as we prayed. Laverne, a woman from the choir, had a lump on her chest, and because of her previous history of cancer, the doctor ordered it removed. Choir members gathered around her one evening, laid hands on her and prayed for God to remove it. The next day, she was on the operating table, already unconscious, ready for surgery when the surgeon admitted he could not find the lump. So they woke her up and sent her home. What a marvelous story of Laverne's faith and the faith of the choir members in God's mercy and power.

Kathy, the 15-year-old daughter of a church member, came to us one morning requesting prayer to remove a cyst or tumor she had on her jawbone, found by X-ray. The youth of the church spent an entire Sunday school hour praying and asking God to heal Kathy. She also came to the women's morning prayer group for anointing and prayer for healing. We laid hands on her and asked God to pour his Holy Spirit through her entire body. When the surgery was done, they found *nothing* where the tumor had been. It was an empty hole. There was not even enough tumor to scrape out for an analysis, and the surgeon was astonished.

Our choir director Jerry Peterson was diagnosed with prostate cancer which had already metastasized into the lymph nodes. He was told that it was very serious and life-threatening. Soon after the diagnosis was made, the ministers of the church and the prayer team plus many other church members, who left work to come, laid hands on Jerry and prayed for his full recovery. Part of the prayer was to order the cancer cells out of Jerry in the name of Jesus and to invite in the healing of the Holy Spirit.

Jerry later reported feeling spiritual energy in the form of heat and electricity traveling through his body, concentrating in the affected area. The surgeon was amazed that he was able to remove the now highly localized tumor so easily. The few affected lymph nodes were also removed, and Jerry has made a complete recovery. It has been five years since the surgery. We found out later that he was not expected to live even one year.

The process of faith healing requires a period of praise and worship which brings us to the awareness of the Holy Spirit in our midst. We usually read Psalm 103 aloud during the worship period. Then hands are laid on the person, and the disease is ordered out in Jesus' name. We are careful to invite in the Holy Spirit to fill the vacancy left by the disease, otherwise the affliction could return. Jesus said, "*When an unclean spirit goes out of a man, he goes through dry places, seeking rest, and finds none. Then he says, 'I will return to my house from which I came.' And when he comes, he finds it empty, swept, and put in order. Then he goes and takes with him seven other spirits more wicked than himself, and they enter and dwell there; and the last state of that man is worse than the first*" (Mt 12:43-45).

Not only are we to cast out physical diseases in Jesus' name, but we are also called on to exorcise spirits of rebellion and confusion from young people. God's power works just as well on spiritual problems as it does on the physical body.

A young woman named Charlene used to live in a constant state of depression. Miriam and I found her with chest pains and nausea one evening at a youth camp where we had gone for a family spiritual retreat. With her permission, we stepped aside from the group and laid healing hands on her, ordering the pain and sickness out of her body in the name of Jesus. Strangely, a deep growl sounded from her chest region, but Charlene didn't hear it. Both Miriam and I felt the moaning sound as it traveled from Charlene's body through our hands and arms into our heads and ears, though no audible sound was heard. We heard it with *spiritual ears.* The long low rumble was repeated twice, then ceased. Charlene immediately perked up, said the pain was gone and she felt fine. This is an example of the evil Satan can inflict on people who are particularly vulnerable. The name of Jesus is a death knell to the forces of evil on this earth.

Increasing numbers of people are becoming ill with unknown diseases. The husband of one of our prayer partners had a mysterious swelling in his body; the minister's wife had a lung disease that was resistant to treatment; a young woman, Gloria, had an abdominal infection that was eating her tissues. We bore down hard in prayer about these things.

It is wonderful to have so many people coming in every day to be prayed for and to help pray for the church and the city. Almost every day the palms of my hands become very hot in the Spirit. Since Jesus laid hands on people, healed them and told us to do the same, we are finding the healing Spirit of God in our *hands.* Two of the three people mentioned above did recover completely, and one only partially.

We have found that injuries due to accidents also succumb to prayers of faith and healing. My friend Robert was building an addition to his house, doing the carpentry work himself, which he loved to do. One morning before leaving for his business, he scampered up a ladder to a scaffold near the ceiling. In his enthusiasm, he struck his head on an open rafter, momentarily passed out and fell backwards to the concrete floor, landing on his back. Regaining consciousness, he realized he couldn't breathe. Air had been completely compressed out of his lungs from the force of the fall. By the time he got his breath, he knew his back had been seriously injured. His wife Gail quickly called an ambulance which rushed him to the emergency room of the hospital. She then called me to pray for him, and I called Miriam.

When I arrived at the emergency room, Robert was lying on a gurney and his face reflected the seriousness of the situation. He thought he had broken his back. We all gathered around him and prayed intensely with tears asking the Lord for healing. When the prayer was finished, I left the hospital feeling at peace about Robert. Sure enough, Robert was released from the hospital the same day and told to rest for a few days because he had chipped a vertebra. He recovered quickly and was soon directing the evangelism committee of the church again. God indeed cares about his servants and is protecting them from the onslaught of evil that seems to be growing stronger and stronger as the end time approaches.

My own body is healing in many ways. Many mornings I waken in the embrace of the Spirit–as though seized by a great and loving power. My insides become hot, and I know healing is taking place throughout my body. Sometimes the Holy Spirit wakens me at night by blowing a strong breath across my face. That is always followed by Spirit heat throughout my body for hours.

The closer I approach to knowledge of the Lord, the fiercer become the attacks of the evil one. Satan is always trying to convince us that we are not healed and God doesn't really care. These attacks usually arrive right after we experience a powerful service of worship during which someone is healed by the loving, healing Spirit of God.

A nagging bladder infection was exerting its fury on my body last week, so I decided to go to a Full Gospel Church Worship service and ask God for healing. The whole congregation came forward to lay hands on me, and I was anointed with oil. The bladder pain ceased and I praised God for healing me.

However, after I came home and went to bed, the pain returned in earnest. I prayed, praised God and claimed healing, but the pain raged on. The evil one would not let go. He kept telling me I was not healed and God didn't care. Then Satan continued by reminding me of some of my recent sins, which I had already confessed and been forgiven for.

Finally, I got up, put on a robe and marched and danced around the house singing God's praises until two A.M. when the pain disappeared completely. Back in bed, I slept soundly and arose the next day totally healed.

One night I was praying earnestly for the reconciliation of a family in our church which was having marital problems when the Holy Spirit came to me with the exquisitely pleasing flower odor, the "Odor of the sweet smell" described by Paul in Philippians. It was the Holy Spirit of God! What a magnificent God!

I am so glad God is for me: *What then shall we say to these things? If God is for us, who can be against us? He who did not spare his own Son, but delivered him up for us all, how shall he not with him also freely give us all things?* (Rom 8:31-32). Otherwise I couldn't survive, for the evil one is attacking fiercely. Twice when I have wakened in pain, the devil has put into my mind that I have a malignancy. He has actually said that word to my consciousness.

One night the pain was in my stomach and another night in my breast where I could feel a lump. I immediately called out "Jesus, Jesus, Jesus" several times. Then peace came, and the Sweet Lord of the Universe said to my spirit, "You do not have cancer. You are mine." The next morning the lump was gone. Praise God! For the longest time, the Holy Spirit filled my whole body with waves of electricity. I felt disconnected from all pain, tension and stress. Indeed, when God is for us, nothing can harm us spiritually.

I decided on one occasion to do an intercession "in extreme," as suggested by John and Paula Sanford in their book, *The Elijah Task*. A man I knew, who lived in another city, was suffering the final stages of a horribly painful cancer. The prayer group had interceded for Marty fervently with tears for a great long time, but he had not improved at all. Neither did he die, but laid there day after day in terrible pain. Finally, I decided that God was keeping Marty alive either because he needed to forgive someone before he died, or he had an unrepentant sin on his conscience. We all knew Marty had given his life to Christ many years ago, but perhaps there was something in his life he had not fully surrendered to God.

With fear and trembling and while pleading for understanding and forgiveness for what I was about to do, I asked God to let me take Marty's spirit on myself. Then I, in Marty's place, asked forgiveness for my/his sins and agreed to forgive everyone who had offended me/him. I asked for the Lord to cover me/him with Jesus' shed blood so that I/he would be forgiven and made acceptable in heaven. Then I asked the Lord to accept him in heaven.

This was not an easy prayer. I was trembling and perspiring heavily. The weight of what I was doing bore my knees into the floor and momentarily I felt the burden of Marty's pain. But when the prayer was finished, that burden was lifted and I felt light again. I quickly asked for Marty's spirit to be returned to him and mine to me. And it was so. Within 24 hours Marty was dead, out of his pain and into the arms of Jesus.

The Scriptural confirmation I found for this procedure was Jesus' own death on the cross in our behalf. He actually took our sins upon himself and our punishment on himself. He also asked us to do the things he did: *"Most assuredly, I say to you, he who believes in me, the works that I do he will do also; and greater works than these he will do, because I go to my Father"* (Jn 14:12). I asked God to bless my prayers and felt no rejection to what I was doing.

Another confirmation of the use of this procedure comes from the lips of Jesus after the Resurrection. *[Jesus] breathed on them, and said to them, "Receive the Holy Spirit. If you forgive the sins of any, they are forgiven them: if you retain the sins of any, they are retained"* (Jn 20:22-23). What a magnificent gift from the God of the Universe to us mortals!

Sometimes God intercedes when the need is urgent and

one's regular prayer partners do not know the danger. One winter day angels worked quickly to save me from a certain accident. Slushy snow had fallen on Saturday, but I was able to get up and down my steep half-mile long hill road because my tires pressed through the slush to grip the pavement.

The next morning I decided I could make it to church the same way. As soon as I started down the hill, I knew it was a mistake. The slush had turned to ice and my car started sliding out of control almost immediately. Ahead was a rather sharp curve to the left which, if I missed, would almost certainly force me into a huge rock beside the road. Momentarily I shuddered at the thought of having to call my insurance agent again and tell him of my latest dumb mistake.

I was praying, pleading for the Lord to save me but continuing to slide inexorably toward that rock and a bashed-in front end. My right front wheel slid over the curb and started down into the ditch, when all at once some huge unseen force shoved my car back onto the road with the front heading straight into the curve. I did not see anything or anyone, but I knew who had put out the order to save and who had fulfilled that order. Angels, unseen angels, had stopped my forward slide and turned the car and the momentum of the slide into another direction. Worship was powerful that day. I continue to thank God and praise him for his tender and watchful care.

One very strange and esoteric example of intercession occurred the following spring. The morning prayer team was deep in prayer when Miriam screamed out with pain in her forehead. She asked us to pray quickly to relieve the hideous pain. Hurriedly we laid our hands on her head asking God to take away the pain, which he did immediately. Miriam said it was one of the worst pains she ever had. We wondered about its source.

An hour later Miriam and I were motoring down a main thoroughfare when an old man drove out of a side street without stopping and slammed into the left door and fender of my car. I had a seat belt on, but my head bounced hard against the side window. The amazing part is that *my head didn't hurt.* The blow on my head was on the left side of my forehead, the same spot where Miriam had received the unknown pain and God's healing. The Lord had allowed Miriam to take my pain because of her love for me. What a wondrous God we have! Perhaps we were allowed to experience this accident to show God's amazing interweaving between physical and spiritual reality.

Our good friend and choir director Jerry Peterson posited a theory that to God all things are happening simultaneously. That would explain the head pain incident. It also illuminates why the Bible is still true and why we receive present-day answers from Scriptures thousands of years old. Even Old Testament passages bring answers to my problems.

Sometimes intercession comes in a negative way. I have been thinking it would become easier to obey the Lord–to keep the commandments and live a holy life as time progressed. But no! The more progress we make toward the kingdom, the more barbs come toward us from the evil one.

This was manifested once when for a two-week period my ears hurt. I had been trying without success to remove from our church building an exercise group using an offshoot of Eastern religious practices. Eastern religions have the philosophy that all people and all life are a part of God and that God does *not* exist as a separate entity. This concept is anathema to the Christian faith. In my attempt to remove this foreign religion from the church building, I made several enemies. When people verbally scourge someone, whether they are present to actually hear the abuse or not, the victim sometimes receives the blows as physical pain in the head or ears.

After two weeks of excruciating ear aches, I consulted the

doctor. He found no cause for the pain but prescribed cortisone drops as temporary relief. They didn't help, but eventually the pain stopped and I knew the talk had ceased.

Sometimes we are called on to intercede in a situation without knowing what it is for. Then we can only pray in the Spirit, allowing God to apply the prayers where they are needed. In the Garden of Gethsemane Jesus told his disciples to wait and pray, but at the time they didn't know what they were to pray for. *"Watch and pray, lest you enter into temptation. The spirit truly is ready, but the flesh is weak"* (Mk 14:38).

In May 1991 the Lord began sending me trembling lips all day. Along with it the patriotic song "America" pressed into my consciousness. So I prayed and prayed all day in the Spirit not knowing what I was interceding for. A few days later the Supreme Court came out with a decision on abortion. They ruled that family planning clinics cannot dispense abortion information. *So* it was that decision they were struggling with the day the Lord called on me to pray all day.

The Lord made me to know that intercessory prayer comes not only from people on earth, from angels and from Jesus, but also from the saints in heaven. One night I was awakened by a male tenor voice calling my name. No one was there, so I looked at the wall where the Lord sometimes sends messages by visions. Light and dark spots appeared on the wall in a confusion of designs, these became the clear picture of a shoe, then walnut shells. When these disappeared, the sparkling jewels of heaven flashed in the room. It was morning before I grasped the meaning of the visions.

When my dear friend Beth died in 1983, she left a message by way of a poem that I should take her discarded shoes as a symbol for finishing the assignment God had for her. The assignment, according to the poem, involved the analogy of harvesting the wrinkled shells of walnuts for some useful purpose.

Here, some ten years after Beth died, a message came from the Lord about Beth. She is in heaven for I saw brightly colored jewels among the shoes and walnut shells, and she still knows and cares about me. No doubt she is praying and interceding for the work I am doing.

How awe-inspiring is God's care for us!

4

Protection

I am becoming increasingly aware of the evil spirits that roam over and rule a large segment of this planet. Jesus called their leader *"the ruler of this world"* (Jn 14:30); the Apostle Paul called them *"rulers of darkness of this age"* (Eph 6:12); and Peter, the disciple, called the devil *"a roaring lion, seeking whom he may devour"* (1 Pet 5:8).

Jesus came to destroy the works of the devil, according to 1 John 3:8. He has given us the tools to accomplish this assignment. Simply speaking his name and asking for a blood covering will scatter these princes of darkness. But it has to be more than lip service. Faith in Jesus and his blood atonement is necessary or we will be defeated, withdrawing naked and wounded.

> *Also there were seven sons of Sceva, a Jewish chief priest, who did so. And the evil spirit answered and said, "Jesus I know, and Paul I know; but who are you?" Then the man in whom the evil spirit was leaped on them, overpowered them, and prevailed*

against them, so that they fled out of that house naked and wounded (Acts 19:14-16).

I began to notice God's continual protection one night in a most unusual place, the bathroom. I couldn't believe my eyes when I saw the flames and flickering of the Holy Spirit in the bathtub! The red flames were easier to see against the white porcelain. "What can this be?" I asked myself. The next day in the utility bathroom, I also saw the flickering of the Holy Spirit. Then I remembered feeling the presence of the Holy Spirit stronger in the bathrooms than anyplace else in the house.

Today the Holy Spirit told me when any orifice of the body is open, evil spirits have access to the body through that orifice so the Spirit is present in private and unexpected places to protect us from evil when we are unclothed and vulnerable.

Genesis tells us God made garments of skins for Adam and Eve to wear after they were removed from Eden, probably to protect them not only from the cold, but also from evil spirits (Gen 3:21). While in the specially protected Garden of Eden there was no need for covering, but afterward much evil was present so protection was needed.

When Jesus sailed across the Sea of Galilee to the country of the Gadarenes, he was met by a naked demoniac. After the demons had been driven out, the demoniac recovered his right mind and put on clothing (Lk 8:26-40). It is logical that demons had convinced him to undress in order for the "legions" of them to enter and take over his body.

In the same way when we see evil, speak of evil or hear evil, that evil agent has access to our bodies through the mouth, nose, eyes or ears. When the mouth and lips are used to sing and praise God, the Holy Spirit comes in by that route. When an organ of the body is used for evil, illness can enter; e.g., cancer, pneumonia, venereal diseases, madness, etc. Illnesses also occur for a number of other reasons, including accidents and generational curses. Very few people are immune to diseases. I also have my share of afflictions.

Breaking God's moral laws, the Ten Commandments (Ex 20), brings physical and spiritual consequences. Keeping Jesus's laws of love described in the Sermon on the Mount (Mt 5-7), brings not only emotional and sometimes physical health, but also unspeakable joy.

When God showed Ezekiel a vision of how to rebuild the temple after the Babylonian captivity, giving detailed instructions to be carried out to the letter, he told Ezekiel to "cover the windows" of the rooms to be used by the priests for changing clothes (Ezek 41:16).

God told Moses to instruct the priests to cover their nakedness with trousers when they ministered to the Lord at the altar. They needed to be safe from evil influences when they were both giving praises to the Lord on behalf of the people and receiving messages from God to give to the people: "*And you shall make for them linen trousers to cover their nakedness; they shall reach from the waist to the thighs*" (Ex 28:42). Today's society could use some advice on covering the body properly and using our God-given organs for good and not evil.

In the same way evil comes in the natural openings of the body. I have actually seen and felt Jesus come into my *eye.* One night I awakened and saw him in the form of a transparent Spirit sitting on the bed next to me. He came closer and closer, then *disappeared into my eye.* While this was happening, my field of vision was like looking at many prisms put together side by side. It felt as though electricity was racing through my entire body and I felt the Holy Spirit's heat in my body for most of that night.

This phenomenon is mysterious and hard to understand, but it is also Scriptural: (Jesus said) "*... even the Spirit of Truth,* *whom the world cannot receive, because it neither sees him nor knows him; but you know him, for he dwells with you and will be in you"* (Jn 14:17).

The evil one uses natural disagreements in a family to initiate strife in the household. When Howard was still alive, we would have terrible stress in the house around Halloween. Evil seems to abound at that time. I remember one Halloween I was so upset and angry that the Lord was cool to me in the night. I asked for forgiveness and resolved to love more. I anointed the house, declared it belonged to Jesus and walked around the entire lot seven times remembering Joshua at Jericho (Josh 6). This prayer and parade never failed to cleanse the house and bring peace.

God himself sends advice and protection at times to keep us from falling into danger. Howard wanted me to go with him to south Texas for a winter vacation two months before he died. I resisted because I felt the Lord did not want me to go. I asked God to make it clear to me whether or not I should go. That very night God relayed a dream with the answer.

In the dream, Howard and I were speeding down the highway at night when suddenly the car lights went out. For what seemed like a long time we were cruising completely blind. Ahead of us was only darkness. Then we approached another car's rear lights and traveled behind it until we came to a filling station where we stopped and fixed the headlights. Starting on, we had driven a short way when the lights went out again, and again we were driving blindly down an unknown, pitch-black highway. The dream ended.

I knew from this that I was not to go with him, but only began to understand it later. When Howard collapsed at home and died instantly, it was confirmation that God wanted to protect me from being present in the car if this had happened during the trip.

We must be constantly vigilant and in touch with God by prayer for our own protection and that of our families. A friend of mine in a nearby town was suffering a long terminal illness and depression was adding to the disease. Frances has since died, but one evening when she was very low, I went to see her, sat on the side of the bed and visited with her for a while. As I drove onto the highway going home, I suddenly felt something clasp my back. Whatever it was had hands which grabbed my neck and began choking me so I couldn't breathe. *Something was trying to kill me!* For a moment I thought, "I'm going to die right here in the middle of the highway and kill others in the process!" I quickly looked for a place to pull over and at the same time started praying in tongues with all the strength I had. Within five seconds the pressure on my throat began to ease and before I had come to a complete stop beside the highway, it was completely gone. Dear God, without your watchful and devoted protection, we would quickly succumb to the forces of darkness of this world.

Just as the Holy Spirit sometimes exudes the "odor of a sweet smell," as described by Paul in Philippians 4:18, evil also has an odor: *But I will remove far from you the northern army, and will drive him away into a barren and desolate land, with his face toward the eastern sea; and his back toward the western sea; his stench will come up and his foul odor will rise, because he has done monstrous things* (Joel 2:20).

The discernment of spirits is one of the nine spiritual gifts listed in 1 Corinthians 12:4-10. Being of scientific leaning, I do not know how to rely on inner prompting about these things, so God has graciously allowed me to see or smell spirits. A crusty street-wise old minister told me one evening that God was giving me a gift. He didn't know what it was, but I would find out, he said. That weekend I was in Missouri visiting my sister when a guest minister laid his hands on my head and told me the same thing. I found out a short time later that the gift God was giving me was the gift of discernment of spirits.

Not long afterward, Miriam and I drove to Eureka Springs, Arkansas, to meet my sister Betty and her husband Jay and to attend the famous Great Passion Play, a story of Jesus' last week on earth before his crucifixion. The discernment of spirits gift came into realization during this trip.

We were eager to get started because June is a beautiful month in the Ozarks. Our drive followed the ribbon of highway around one mountain, over another, precariously bisecting a saddle connecting other mountains until it dropped steeply into a valley to cross a stream. We came to a small town where a rustic stand offering blueberries for sale nestled comfortably in a school yard beside the highway. We stopped to sample the tender sweet berries which seemed particularly delicious because they had been grown on rocky hillsides under the flaming Arkansas sun. Indeed, they were so good we bought a gallon each to take home and freeze.

As we drove on, we noticed wild roses gracing the highway berm, and also colorful gaillardia or Indian blanket wildflowers weaving bright red and yellow threads through the pure white Queen Ann's lace. The blue-gray haze of distant mountains gave us a sense of visual eternity, refreshment and peace.

But even this beautiful world God has made and blessed has its enemies. Arriving at the motel, I felt a compulsion to hurry to the room, so I charged on ahead of the others. But for some strange reason, the key wouldn't open the lock. I saw the cleaning maid just about to disappear around the corner, so I rushed after her and asked her to help me open the lock. There was a great reluctance on her part to come, but I was insistent. She took my key and opened the lock easily. I was a little embarrassed at my stupidity, but I did warmly thank her and added a "God bless you."

As I walked back down the hallway to get my luggage, I smelled a terrible stench. It was very putrid and I shook my head from side to side to get away from it. It seemed heavy and thick, a choking odor that smelled slightly sulphur-like.

Later I told this story to Miriam who said she saw the cleaning maid as I was hurrying to the room and sensed evil in her. Later we saw this same woman and she looked clean and pure to our spiritual eyes. Possibly some evil spirit had attached itself to her, but when I asked God's blessing on her, that blessing had stripped the evil spirit from her and left her clean. The evil I smelled was the disembodied demon spirit loosed from her body and having no place to go. Being out in the world these days requires one to be watchful and in constant communion with God.

5

Jay

My sister's husband Jay was a sturdy specimen of manhood. He stood five feet ten inches tall and was solid muscle, acquired by working hard all his life. At 17 he had joined the U.S. Marines and after training was sent to Corregidor. Captured when the Japanese took over Bataan, he spent three wretched years in a prison camp.

The latter years of his life were cut short because of the starvation and suffering he experienced there. He never learned to hate during that period of his life, but he did learn to swear. Such words came easily to him all his life.

Because he saw so much suffering in the prison camp, Jay decided to give his life to relieving suffering. After he married Betty, he attended veterinary college and became an accomplished veterinarian. They settled in a small Missouri town where he made a fine living treating livestock and there they raised two sons, both of whom were successful in their fields of endeavor.

Jay's life rocked along pretty normally until after he retired when he began to have visual problems due to diabetes. A few years later, his heart began to falter and in May 1991 cancer was discovered in one kidney. It was after the cancer surgery that Betty and I began in earnest to witness to him about salvation in Christ.

We thought he was a believer, but he didn't want to discuss it. He did, however, ask me to pray for him before the surgery and God brought him through the operation alive.

Three months later Jay's heart began to fail again. I asked the Lord if he were going to take him, and God said, "Yes." I asked him if Jay would go to heaven, and he said, "I will deal gently with him for Betty's sake." *Believe on the Lord Jesus Christ and you will be saved, you and your household* (Acts 16:31).

On the first of September, Jay was in the hospital with his heart failing when the Lord sent a hymn with the words, "The Master has come and he calls us to follow the path of his footsteps he leaves on the way." He kept sending this until I realized I must do what Jesus would do – drive to Springfield, lay hands on Jay and pray.

This was not easy to do for he was a strong-willed man who, except for his prison-camp days, had always been in control of his life. But I did go and he was willing to have me pray for him.

When I returned home, the Lord sent the strangest song to mind. It is frequently sung at weddings and the words run: "... woman takes life from a man and gives it back again." It seemed the message was that I had taken life from Jesus and given it to Jay. Praise Jesus and praise God! I knew then I must write a letter to Jay to say all the things I was afraid to say with people present.

Dear Jay,

Rejoice! The Lord told me last night he was restoring you to life for a while in order that you could learn more about him before he takes you. He has carefully looked after you all your life and wants you to know him.

His plan for people is that they live the best they can under his dominion. But even when we live the best we can, we still do things we shouldn't. He says you need to ask forgiveness for those things, then forget them and try to live every day as a fresh new gift from him. He sent Jesus to take your punishment for past sins so you need not bear them. He says you should give him all your worries and problems and praise him and thank him for this life. He says whenever you get into trouble, just call upon the name of Jesus – not as a swear word, but as a request. He says to use the phrase "God bless" instead of cursing. He is preparing you a place in heaven with him, but he cannot have cursing in his house.

He says he knows you and loves you more than anyone else ever has or ever could. You are special to him – and you are special to all of your family also. Consider all the concerned people at your bedside and calling on the phone. Your children love you also, and your wife prays for you every day because she loves you.

Give thanks to God every day you are allowed to live. Smile and laugh a lot and enjoy every day. This universe is not just a freak of nature and some uncaring power. There is a loving God, a meaning and purpose to life, which we must learn and love.

Your loving sister-in-law,
Dottie

A few nights later, the Lord sent a contemporary song with the line, "He can make a perfect heart," to my consciousness to tell me God is willing to heal Jay's heart. Then God said, "He has humbled himself before me." Hurray! Jay has met the Lord and will have a place in heaven! He has prayed to God, and God has forgiven him.

I received a call a few days later that Jay was back in the hospital with heart and kidney failure. The Lord sent the hymn

"There is power in the blood" all night, so I prayed for Jay, asking that his sins be covered by the blood of Christ and that his heart and kidneys be healed. I know a young minister who says he always prays for life for the sick. God can make whatever decision he wants, but Jesus prayed for a more abundant *life* for all of us (Jn 10:10), and that is a good model to follow.

Betty's minister visited Jay in the hospital and Jay declared his faith in Christ to her. Praise God! He improved enough to go home and Betty reported he was sleeping better. Jay lived three more years, much of it riding an old tractor over his farm checking on the cattle, fishing in the small lake and watching the seasons change. A brown mongrel dog followed him everywhere he went and was inconsolable when he died.

His amazing strength was demonstrated one afternoon when I was visiting. He decided to build an electric fence to keep the heifers away from the herd. Betty and I were convinced he did not have strength to do this alone, so we volunteered to help. Jay paced off the ten yards between posts while Betty and I pounded them in with a post-maul. We put all our strength into it, but the small metal post would only go in an inch or two at a time. Finally Jay told us to move out of the way, took the maul, gave it a mighty thrust and the post sank into the ground as though through sand.

Three months later the Lord took him quickly and quietly while Betty was at work. His funeral was the talk of the town as many townspeople and farmers people crowded in, overflowing the small funeral home. Someone said "There isn't one here he didn't cuss out," but they knew he had saved many of their farm animals, going above and beyond normal practice. They also knew he was without pretense. He was inside what he appeared to be outside.

When Sandy Meredeth, a young teenager with a high clear soprano voice, sang "One day at a time, sweet Jesus, that's all

I'm asking of you ..." there wasn't a dry eye in the house.

After he died, the Lord showed me he was in heaven, the land that is very far off. I saw Jay as a young man with bright eyes and a smile. He looked so happy and content. The Lord did add that there was a restriction on him there. Though I don't know for sure, I couldn't help but think he may not be allowed to speak until he learns not to swear.

6

A Warning

What strange and frightening visions came to me in September 1991. For several nights running I wakened in the Spirit and with eyes closed saw a fabric screen. I did not understand the three images on it except for an eye that was always on the left side. The images were small, and there was always much screen in-between. Since no message came through, I decided to open my eyes and look for a visual message.

Some kind of activity started showing on a corner of the wall, but a message did not register. Then a great cluster of lines of light burst out of that activity and fanned along the wall and across the ceiling as though they were going to either come to me or go over my head. They disappeared and in the original spot I saw red and white stripes and white stars on a blue field, a symbol of America. This flag sank into the ground out of my sight.

I sprang wide awake with the impact of what I had seen. The Holy Spirit placed in my mind an immediate interpretation. *The United States is going to be destroyed by atomic missiles.* Those very missiles I saw in detailed visions the following night after asking God to confirm the message.

One vision was a box of tiny balls – atoms, no doubt. The next was a bomb-shaped image filled with tiny balls, and the third was a great explosion! Fire spread all over the wall! There can be no doubt that America is to be attacked, but the question is – *When?* Could it be the beginning of the tribulation or sooner? I shook with the realization of what God had given me. "Please," I said, "please, Lord, confirm this to me."

Taking my Bible in hand – the pages I have wept over, laughed over, received inspiration, instructions and chastisement from – I opened it where I hoped the Lord wanted it to open. By chance I opened to the fourth chapter of Esther where she was warned about the coming destruction of the Jews. My heart sank. I said, "Lord, do it again," and again opened my Bible by chance. The second time the Bible opened to Proverbs 22:21, *That I may make you know the certainty of the words of truth ....* The third time it opened to Ezekiel 35:5, *"Because you have ... shed the blood of children ...."* Everyone is laughing and partying and making plans for the next generation, not realizing the danger that will come to all the earth's children after the Rapture. "What must I do, Lord?" I asked. The Bible opened to Jeremiah 9:20-22: *Yet hear the Word of the Lord, O women, and let your ear receive the word of his mouth; teach your daughters wailing and everyone her neighbor a lamentation. For death has come through our windows, has entered our palaces to kill off the children – no longer to be outside; and the young men – no longer on the streets! Speak, thus says the Lord: "Even the carcasses of men shall fall as refuse on the open field like cuttings after the harvester, and no one shall gather them."*

Can there be a more accurate description of the effects of atomic radiation?

For several days after this revelation I had the feeling the Lord was trying to tell me something, perhaps give me an assignment. Several times on opening the Bible, I found it to be Zephaniah 1:4 *"I will stretch out my hand against Judah and against all the inhabitants of Jerusalem ...."*

Again the Bible opened to the first chapter of Jeremiah where God commissions Jeremiah to speak for the Lord to tell the people what is to happen to them if they do not change their ways. *"For you shall go to all to whom I send you, and whatever I command you, you shall speak .... Behold, I have put my words in your mouth .... I will utter my judgments against them concerning all their wickedness, because they have forsaken me, burned incense to other gods, and worshiped the works of their own hands. Therefore prepare yourself and arise, and speak to them all that I command you."*

Then the Lord sent a vision of a hand holding a pencil and a person's head stuck out of a broken window. The interpretation is that I am to write God's message to the people–a call to repentance and a warning that tragedy and destruction are to come if we don't change our ways.

With the Lord's warnings ringing in my ears and his clear instructions in my heart, I wrote the following open letter to the people of America and mailed it to 20 major newspapers throughout the United States. On the way to the post office, I became apprehensive about sticking my neck out in this manner. I switched on the car radio and heard a minister say, "When the Lord tells you to do something, don't worry about your feelings. Just make certain it is Scriptural and proceed." So I did.

An Open Letter to the American People

To the editor,

In ancient times when people were straying from God's ordinances for right living, a prophet was sent to call them back. If they did return, God restored them to peace and security, but when they didn't, he punished them severely.

The time has come for a prophet to appear again and speak to America. He would speak for the Lord and say, "Return, o my people, to the mind-set of your founding fathers who sailed to these shores to worship the God of the Lord Jesus Christ freely. They came to worship and serve God in this clean new land that I provided. I have been very patient with this nation because I planted you in an abundance of resources to live in peace and to learn to know me, to love me and to serve me. But you have preferred to forget me and serve yourselves.

"Every year you have sacrificed one-and-a-half million of your unborn children on the altar of expediency. You have practiced promiscuity with your bodies and encouraged your children to do the same, flaunting my rule of one man for one woman. You have even refused to be what I made you, whether male or female. You have withheld your hand in training your children by example, correction and discipline in faith in the God of Jesus Christ and moral living, allowing their tongues to blaspheme, and their bodies and minds to be poisoned by alcohol, drugs and pornography. You have allowed them to be their own gods and do their own thing, following your example.

"You have brought into your house newspapers, magazines, television programs and books that exalt evil, violence and atheism. You have promoted discord, disunity and violence in your families and abused and neglected your aged ones. You have not exercised true and swift justice in your courts as was the intention of your ancestors. You have spoken, published and practiced lies in every aspect of your lives: family, business, education, industry and government. You have been exploiters instead of keepers and guardians of your planet. You have failed to give me the first tithe of your labor. You have even failed to acknowledge my dominion over you.

> "I created this nation, guided its formation, delivered it from oppression, preserved it from destruction and maintained its freedom. But with that freedom you have chosen evil. I have forgiven you and called you back many times, and you have returned. Even now, it is not too late. Come back to the Hebrew-Christian faith of your ancestors, live in true justice and righteousness and I will again come to your aid. Cease and desist from these terrible things you are doing and return to me. Return to faith in me and in your Savior, Jesus Christ, who died that you might live.
>
> "If you do not, I will allow you to be destroyed. I will cut off the rains and snows upon which you depend for your food and even your drinking water. I will allow great earthquakes, fires and diseases to buffet you. I will allow you to be wiped out with your own technology in the hands of your enemies. I will allow your cities and your abundance of things to be destroyed until you are stripped naked before me and beg for mercy. The time is very short. Return to me, and I will save you," says the Lord.

It was a great disappointment to me that no newspaper printed this letter, as far as I know. But I was obedient to the Lord and put out the warning. While writing it, I had no idea when this attack was to come. But I persisted in the question of: When, Lord, when?

For a number of months the Lord was silent concerning this request. Then one night either when I was about to go to sleep or just after a light early sleep, the Lord wakened me and I was in the Spirit. With eyes closed I saw a blank screen with an eye on the right side. An atomic mushroom cloud appeared in the middle of the screen; that disappeared, then a cluster of mushroom clouds appeared all over the screen. As the meaning of these visions pressed into my consciousness, I gasped. *"It is really going to happen!"* I said to myself. "This nation is going to be destroyed by atomic bombs coming in as missiles!"

The Lord was not finished with the message, for the next night, the visions continued as though uninterrupted. I saw huge cities being completely destroyed. I saw great mounds of rubble that once had been beautiful buildings intended for business, medicine, education and worship. The Holy Spirit told me these were *our cities.* I shook and wept.

The next day I went about my chores in a daze, realizing that God had told me something that felt like honey to the mouth but bitter in the belly. It was sweet in the mouth because *God* had spoken to me, but bitter in the belly because it was a message no one wanted to hear or would accept.

> *And I went to the angel and said to him, "Give me the little book." And he said to me, "Take and eat it; and it will make your stomach bitter, but it will be as sweet as honey in your mouth." And I took the little book out of the angel's hand and ate it, and it was as sweet as honey in my mouth. But when I had eaten it, my stomach became bitter. And he said to me, "You must prophesy again about many peoples, nations, tongues and kings"* (Rev 10:9-11).

Also,

> *Now when I looked, there was a hand stretched out to me; and behold a scroll of a book was in it ... and written on it were lamentations and mourning and woe ... and he said ... "fill your stomach with this scroll ..." And it was in my mouth like honey in sweetness* (Ezek 2:9–3:3).

Not long after that the Lord wakened me at night and said, *"At the turn of the century."* I sat up in bed and said the phrase over and over, trying to get my understanding to catch up with my ears.

So God has established the time of this destruction and is sending out a warning. This prophecy matches very well the prophecies in my previous book *These Last Days* in which God told me on the eighth day of January 1991 that this is *the last decade* before the Lord comes. We know from Revelation that the earth is not going to be a pleasant place to be during the tribulation which follows. Though nobody knows the day or hour of Christ's return, as he said in Matthew 24:36, we certainly know the season. The preliminaries he spoke about in Matthew 24 have happened and are happening. I believe Jesus is coming for the Church very soon. All the prophecies I have received from God indicate it is to be around the turn of the century.

I asked for a confirmation on the timing of the attack on America, and the Bible opened by chance to the second chapter of Isaiah which describes *The Day of the Lord* in which people hide from the terror of the Lord by going into holes in the rocks. Another confirmation of the timing message came the next day when I was reading a newspaper article about the Sutton Avian Research Center, and the phrase *"at the turn of the century"* stuck out at me as though in bold letters. These were the exact words God had given me.

Though I asked God what to do with this information, I already knew that it must be published. In Ezekiel God said:

> *"Son of man, I have made you a watchman for the house of Israel; therefore hear a word from my mouth, and give them warning from me: When I say to the wicked, 'You shall surely die,' and you give him no warning, nor speak to warn the wicked from his way, to save his life, that same wicked man shall die in his iniquity; but his blood I will require at your hand. Yet, if you warn the wicked, and he does not turn from his wickedness, nor from his wicked way, he shall die in his iniquity; but you have delivered your soul"* (3:17-19).

I know my assignment from the Lord is to make known the prophecies he gives me. God loves me and has plans for my entire life of service to him. The thought is thrilling, but frightening, because these assignments will probably go against the grain of society and will be ridiculed, and I may be persecuted, hated and threatened. I feel like Jeremiah, the weeping prophet. I want to raise my head in the joy of the Lord, but there is great judgment and destruction to come.

7

Miracles

One of the simplest forms of miracles is a pattern of coincidences that seems to be beyond normal expectancy. One Christmas season, several dove-tail experiences ensued that show God's continual working in our lives.

It started with a Sunday school party we were to attend after Saturday night church services. The phone rang just as we were deciding not to go to the party because I had forgotten to prepare a dish to take. It was my friend Miriam asking if we were going to the party. When I said we weren't going because I didn't have anything to take, she offered a plate of freshly baked cookies. So we went with Miriam's cookies in our hands.

The next day I made chocolate chip cookies in preparation for Christmas, and just as they were coming out of the oven, a neighbor from across the street stopped in. He ate two or three cookies and seemed to enjoy them so much I offered him a plate of cookies to take home. He looked surprised, laughed, and said, "I asked my wife this morning to make chocolate chip cookies and she said she didn't have time." He took them.

The next day was Christmas Eve and for some strange reason, when I made rolls for Christmas dinner, I made two pizza pans full, 60 rolls, when one would have been plenty for our company dinner. Just then Miriam called saying she had an oven fire and it had taken two hours to clean the oven. She didn't know, she added, what she was going to do for bread for her family Christmas dinner. Bingo! I took her the extra pizza pan of rolls. Thank you, Father, for watching over every detail of our lives so carefully and completely.

We find that many miracles happen when we follow God's instructions in our lives. Paul wrote in 1 Thessalonians 5:17, *Pray without ceasing*, and in Ephesians 6:18, *Praying always with all prayer and supplication ....*

I discovered the value of praying without ceasing one day while driving to Missouri to see my family. During the drive I talked to the Lord as though he were sitting in the next seat, sang praises, hymns and recited memorized Psalms, which are prayers in verse. Along one stretch of a two-lane highway, a pickup truck met me, flinging a stone into my windshield. A star-shaped break appeared, radiating short lines in all directions. I thought, "Oh, oh, that crack will probably continue to lengthen, and I'll have to replace the windshield." Then I returned to prayer and Psalms. Two days later I washed the windshield, and it was perfectly clear. No crack and no lines. Wow! The power of the spoken Word of God is beyond the imagination of mortals.

The trip to Missouri was to check on my brother Basil who was reported to have a block in blood circulation to his foot. He was scheduled to go to the hospital the following Monday for examination and possible amputation. I met our sister Betty at Basil's house, for we had agreed to pray together for the foot. It didn't look very promising. His right foot was white and blue, and we could detect no pulse. Basil was eager to try anything to save his foot so he accepted with tears our offer of prayer. We then took turns massaging the foot and leg, praying silently for about half an hour. As we prayed, the foot began to lose the bluish-white appearance and look more alive, but we didn't know for sure what had happened. The doctor checked it on Monday and was amazed at the spontaneous change. No amputation was necessary. God had restored circulation to his foot! Praise to our God of mercy!

Miracles happen in the world of nature also. God has given us a method to use in dispelling storms. He demonstrated it when he and the disciples were in a boat on the Sea of Galilee: *Then he (Jesus) arose and rebuked the wind, and said to the sea, "Peace, be still!" And the wind ceased and there was a great calm. But he said to them, "Why are you so fearful? How is it that you have no faith?"* (Mk 4:39-40).

It was an early May morning. Howard and I had just moved to Circle Mountain and were having breakfast in front of our big picture window with its view of the beautiful Sand Creek valley to the west. A storm was beginning to appear on the horizon and it looked very black. Storms that strike in the morning are rare but can be severe. We watched as it continued to darken and approach very quickly, we thought. Then I remembered Jesus stilling the waves on the Sea of Galilee and calling for his disciples to have faith. I also remembered Jesus saying to his disciples: *"And whatever you ask in my name, that I will do, that the Father may be glorified in the Son"* (Jn 14:13).

We were in a vulnerable position perched on the top of a cliff overlooking the river valley. I suppose it would not have been necessary to go outside, but I did. I pointed my finger toward the storm and said emphatically, "I command you, in the name of Jesus, to cease and desist! Father, I ask you to take your mighty hand and flatten this storm, take the danger out of it and leave us with a gentle rain."

As we continued to watch, the storm clouds lightened and turned toward the north circumventing the city. Next they moved around to the east, then south. A gentle rain backed up to us from the south soaking the earth with much needed moisture. No storm hit anyplace in the vicinity that day.

What a powerful tool to use for the good of people! Jesus said to have faith in God: *So Jesus answered and said to them, "Have faith in God. For assuredly, I say to you, whoever says to this mountain, 'Be removed and be cast into the sea' and does not doubt in his heart, but believes that those things he says will come to pass, he will have whatever he says"* (Mk 11:22-23). A weak, indecisive faith won't do it. Our faith must be strong and confident to ask for and expect miracles.

One of the most awe-inspiring miracles of my entire life happened last spring. This most amazing gift from the Lord happened during the high school graduation of my sister's grand-daughter. I was traveling to Missouri with storm warnings in my ears and apprehension in my heart. Passing Joplin and heading for Springfield, I saw dark, wicked looking clouds to the north. I started to pray both in tongues and in English, and the clouds faded somewhat.

About ten miles north of Springfield, the rain started, but it was not heavy or violent. However, after I arrived safely at Betty's, the rain became a torrent. Praise the Lord for saving me from driving through it. It continued to rain moderately until we went to the high school gymnasium for Jamie's graduation ceremony. While we were there, a fierce lightning storm hit with heavy rain and hail. This lasted for almost two hours while the ceremony was proceeding.

I prayed throughout the ritual for the safety of this assembly, for tornadoes were forecast. We stayed in the gymnasium for an extra half-hour waiting for the rain to stop, but it didn't. The electricity went off, and we decided to go to the car. As we hurried across ditches and rough ground, I noticed we were walking through deep puddles of water, but my feet didn't feel the shock of cold water pouring over the tops of my dress shoes. Betty said the puddles were four to six inches deep, and when we reached the car everyone had shoes, stockings and feet that were soaking wet.

The amazing part is – *my feet* didn't get wet, and neither did *my shoes!* I must have been protected by angels going before me. Needless to say, I didn't tell anyone about this and I even hesitant to put it in this book. I do not deserve this special treatment, but I am so thankful for God's continual and loving care of me. He has told me when I step out for him and remain obedient, he will do for me things I cannot do for myself.

My friend Miriam tells an even stranger story of God's producing a business, placing it where it was needed at the time, then causing it to disappear. She was riding in an automobile across the wide expanse of western Kansas with her daughter-in-law and a small baby. The motel they had planned to stay in had confused their reservation number, so they continued on.

It was the middle of the night when they noticed they were getting low on gasoline, and there was not another town for at least 60 miles. Fearful of becoming stalled on a dark lonely highway, they began to pray earnestly and continuously for God's help. Their gas gauge was registering empty and had been for some time. All they saw ahead was the tunnel of light made by their headlights and those of occasional oncoming vehicles. Terror began to play at the corners of their consciousness. What kind of crazy person might be prowling the highways at night to prey upon two helpless women and a baby?

They had all but given up hope of avoiding disaster when they saw a light shine out of the dark night. An exit appeared off the main highway at that point, so they quickly turned and drove toward the light. To their immense relief, they saw it was a small service station. A single attendant on duty commented that from the sound of the tank when he started putting in gasoline, they must have been driving on fumes. They already knew that. With many prayers of thanksgiving to God, they drove on to the next town where they found a motel in which to spend the rest of the night.

The amazing part of the story is they never saw this station again, though they have made many trips along that particular stretch of Kansas highway. They watch every year, trying to locate it, but it is completely gone, leaving no trace.

In a similar vein, I have seen God increase food to cover the number of people to be fed, just as Jesus did when he multiplied five loaves and two fishes to feed thousands (Mk 6:32-44). Our church sponsors block parties around town, especially for the unchurched families in our city. We offer them hot dogs, lemonade and cookies, a clown ministry, music and Jesus.

The first party we held attracted a crowd of 200, mostly children. Someone had brought a small pan of chili as garnish for hot dogs. Everyone, it seemed, wanted chili sauce on his hot dog. We kept dipping a spoon of chili on each child's hot dog, and the Lord kept replenishing the pan of chili until we used the last spoon of chili on the last hot dog. We all agreed it was a miracle. Everyone knew there was not enough chili sauce to cover 200 hot dogs, but the Lord multiplied the chili to garnish every one.

The Bible tells us the Lord not only multiplies things that are needed, but he also takes away unneeded things. This occurred when Jesus caused the boat in which he was riding on the Sea of Galilee to be at the shore immediately, without the passage of any time: *But he [Jesus] said to them, "It is I; do not be afraid." Then they willingly received him into the boat, and immediately the boat was at the land where they were going* (Jn 6:20-21).

One winter in south Texas, Howard had driven our dirty camper into a manual carwash. I like to operate the water spray wand so I washed the camper that day. Midway around the camper, I glanced down at my clothes, and it looked as though I had been in a mud fight. There were mud spots and streaks all over my white blouse, jeans and white tennis shoes. I was going to be filthy when finished, but it would be worth it to have a clean camper.

When I was through I got in the camper to change clothes and saw, to my complete astonishment, that my blouse, jeans and tennis shoes were absolutely clean! The mud spots were gone and there was no trace of them having been there! How thrilled I was at this simple example of the Lord's care of us. He is interested in the smallest detail of our lives and often helps us even before we know to ask.

Since Howard died, the Lord has been careful to give me advice about home repair and maintenance that women normally don't think about. One night he sent a vision of the bricks in my house crumbling and falling out of the wall. The dream was quite vivid, and I remembered it in detail when I wakened. I wondered what the dream meant. Then I remembered Howard having the bricks painted with a water sealant after we moved in the house because, he said, used bricks crumble with the freezing and thawing of winter. It had been five years since that brick treatment had been applied, so I decided the Lord was telling me to have it done again. I did, thanking the Lord, my adviser, my counsellor, my friend.

In the same manner, one summer day the Lord sent the Christmas song about Santa Claus and reindeer with the words,

"Up on the housetop, clop, clop, clop ..." I ignored it for a while, thinking my mind was playing some kind of out-of-season joke, but the song persisted. Finally I decided to look at the roof of my house. Sure enough, limbs of the sycamore tree were so close to the roof, the next strong wind would cause them to flog the roof, possibly breaking shingles. I got help to trim off the limbs. Still the song would not go away, so the next morning I checked the front of the house, cutting off oak limbs that were too near the roof.

The third morning, the song was still persisting so I took my bird-watching binoculars outside and examined the roof shingle by shingle. There, on the very peak of the roof were a number of upraised shingles, the result of an 80 mph wind that had occurred a few days before. The night after getting the roof repaired, a heavy rain fell, but I was protected because of the loving and ever-constant care of the Lord.

A weird and esoteric incident occurred one day when Miriam and I were anointing a new house for protection and asking God's blessings on whoever came in. Miriam was using Jordan River water she had brought from Israel. Holding the bottle in her right hand, with the left hand she carefully dipped in the water and touched every door, window and major piece of furniture. We prayed in every room and when finished, she exclaimed that her *right hand* was wet in the palm. In the midst of deep and fervent prayer, the very physical glass container had de-materialized, allowing water to seep through.

There is a mysterious, mystical truth in this phenomenon. It seems that in the presence of pure Spirit, matter disappears. Physicists have long known that matter, as solid as it seems, consists of great expanses of space tied together by particles of energy. Perhaps in the strong presence of God's Holy Spirit, the energy God relays to physical matter is withdrawn.

This is how the kingdom of heaven is going to come about here on earth. When all people have reached a state of complete holiness by the admission of Jesus into their lives, the old flawed world that Satan controls will disappear and the new spiritual heaven and earth will emerge. They will be so perfect there will be no place for evil: *And I saw a new heaven and a new earth, for the first heaven and the first earth had passed away ... And God will wipe away every tear from their eyes; there shall be no more death, nor sorrow nor crying; and there shall be no more pain, for the former things have passed away. Then he who sat on the throne said, "Behold, I make all things new ..."* (Rev 21:1,4-5). I remember receiving a vision in which God showed me two identical scenes superimposed on each other: one was ordinary life as we know it, and the other beside it was colorful, brilliant and perfect. The brilliant one represented a part of the new spiritual earth that is the visual manifestation of God's perfection with no evil in it: The Land That Is Very Far off.

Another incident occurred one night when I wakened in the spirit and saw a brilliant day-like scene out my bedroom window. The grass was a sparkling emerald green, the apple tree appeared in its proper place with a birdbath underneath. Everything was so beautiful. Around the birdbath, flowers were blooming in glorious color. The whole scene took on a quality of reality I'd never witnessed before. I sat up in bed, engrossed in the beauty before me in the middle of a very dark night. I saw, as it were, a window blind rolling down, closing off this awesome scene and leaving me again in the dark night of present reality in this world that evil dominates. *Jesus said "I will no longer talk much with you, for the ruler of this world is coming, and he has nothing in me"* (Jn 14:30).

The application of this miracle to present life comes in many ways, one of which is in baptism. When a convert is baptized, either by immersion or sprinkling or pouring, and when intense and fervent prayer accompanies the baptism, skin and flesh can become spiritual so that some molecules of baptismal water, which has become sanctified through prayer, may seep through the skin into every cell, thereby cleansing it of all evil and purifying the entire body for service for the Lord. Dear God, could this scenario be the truth you intended for us to experience?

This is really the explanation of all miracles. In the presence of fervent prayer, natural physical life diminishes and can even disappear, transporting the person or event into the new realm of the kingdom of heaven where there is only perfection: thus, a healed body, a flattened storm, abundant food or water for a hungry crowd, resurrection for a dead body or a dead spirit.

An amazing incident of flesh becoming transparent in the presence of pure Spirit happened to a youth at a Day Spring retreat two years ago. Fifteen-year-old Nathan was grieving over the death of his younger brother, a hemophiliac, who was twelve years old when taken. Nathan felt responsible, somehow, for his brother's demise. In the midst of a powerful service of praise and worship in an outdoor amphitheater at night, Nathan was taken out of his body to the very gates of heaven where he saw Jesus with his dead brother. His brother was smiling and looked so happy. He spoke to Nathan and told him it was all right and he should stop worrying.

The next thing Nathan knew, he was back on the ground in his body, *but he could see everything, even with his eyes closed.* His eyelids had become transparent in the presence of pure Spirit, and the darkness of night had vanished. Light was everywhere. See Psalm 139:11b, *Even the night shall be light about me.*

This comes under the same category as Moses' glowing face reflecting the Holy Spirit of God within him. His flesh had become transparent, allowing the children of Israel to see God's glory in his body: *Now it was so, when Moses came down from Mount Sinai ... that Moses did not know that the skin of his face shone while he talked with him.... And whenever the children of Israel saw the face of Moses, that the skin of Moses' face shone, then Moses would put the veil on his face again, until he went in to speak with him* (Ex 34:29-35). The Spirit of God was so intensely present in Moses' body that the glow of that Spirit shone through flesh made transparent in the presence of pure, sanctified Spirit.

Sometimes the miracles God performs are so simple and so uplifting they cry out to be told. Jesus came that *every living thing* might have abundant life: *"I have come that they may have life, and that they may have it more abundantly"* (Jn 10:10). This includes plants and animals.

This principle came to me clearly one year when a man with a grudge and a chain saw cut a deep groove completely around the trunk of a beautiful sugar maple tree. The tree belonged to his neighbor, but it shed leaves on his property. We could see the groove, and it appeared to be about an inch deep, well through the cambium layer. The tree grew across the street from my cousin Dorothy's house so she and I laid hands on that butchered tree and prayed for its survival. Then we waited.

We waited and waited. Summer passed and the tree was still green and beautiful. Autumn arrived and the leaves turned the most beautiful shades of red and yellow, even more beautiful than any other maple tree in the neighborhood. It has been three years since the tree was butchered, but God refused to let it die. It grows larger and prettier every year. God does care about the entire creation and is actively working for abundant life for all.

8

Personal Instructions

There was not another vehicle on the road that summer afternoon as I aimed my car at the horizon and shifted my mind toward the prairie on either side and the sky above.

Scissortail flycatchers and grasshopper sparrows perched on the fences, wild sunflowers crowded the ditches and cattle grazed on the abundant prairie grasses. The canopy of sky displayed long streaks of thin clouds which looked as though they had been combed by a giant hand.

There was such a peace enveloping me, a confidence that my journey, not only today, but all days, was straight, paved and guarded by him into whose hands I had committed my life. I would make a conscious decision to fill every moment with the joy of the Lord as the Apostle Paul did when he sang God's praises while sitting in a Philippian prison. Paul was hungry, cold, sick, bleeding and in pain from beatings. But his sins prior to conversion had been forgiven, and since then he was innocent of violence or crime against anyone. At that moment, he burst into songs of praises to the One in whose care he had really lived, whose grace was sufficient for all his needs (2 Cor 12:9), and who planned and supervised all his days.

I decided right then, at post 17 of County Route 6, to be joyful for all things: loneliness, widowhood, high blood pressure and the various pains and ailments of advancing age. God was sufficient for me in the past, is in the present and will be sufficient in my future. My happiness would not depend on circumstances, but on salvation in Christ.

Not many months after Howard died, the Lord sent a vision of a drawer full of pencils. There seemed to be no end of pencils. The next day, I looked at Howard's drawer of pencils and decided the Lord was telling me to do something constructive with them. At the same time, I thought about my closets full of clothing and started taking some of them to the Salvation Army. But even that was not the purpose of the vision.

A few days later I visited an empty warehouse where a dedicated young woman was attempting to start a rescue mission. Anna was sitting on a desk in a cold office, bundled in a coat, looking as though she had been told to prepare dinner for 20 people but had no food in the house. That was almost literally the situation. God had told her to start a rescue mission, but she had no resources except this unheated warehouse for which someone had donated a down payment. I had read about it in the papers and had come to give her a small check. Casually, I asked her what was needed to start the mission. She blinked, gulped, and said, "Fifty thousand dollars."

That was when I blinked and gulped. I gave her the small check, turned and went home. As I drove up the hill, the Lord brought to mind the drawer of pencils again. It was then I realized the main thrust of the vision was not the pencils but the inheritance I had received from my hard-working husband. From that moment I knew I was to use the deposit box of stock certificates to help Anna build a rescue mission.

God brought to mind the passage in Isaiah: *"Is this not the fast that I have chosen; to loose the bonds of wickedness, to undo the heavy burdens, to let the oppressed go free, and that you break every yoke? Is it not to share your bread with the hungry, and that you bring to your house the poor who are cast out; when you see the naked, that you cover him, and not hide yourself from your own flesh?"* (58:6-7).

A similar passage appears in Matthew when Jesus said, *"Then the king will say to those on his right hand, 'Come you blessed of my Father, inherit the kingdom prepared for you from the foundation of the world: for I was hungry and you gave me food, I was thirsty and you gave me drink; I was a stranger and you took me in ...' "* (25:34-35).

It might be dangerous to bring the homeless into my house, but I could help build a shelter close to the downtown area where the homeless poor could rest, recover and regain hope to find work, an apartment and a new life.

The construction took several months and much more money than the original estimate, but churches and civic organizations contributed plus many private individuals. The Lighthouse Rescue Mission has been in full operation now for three years, keeping from ten to forty people every day. Many times whole families with children take shelter for a few days or weeks. God is the one who directs the work and the length of stay. A spirit of acceptance and love greets the stranger at the door and permeates the whole building. A sign on the wall quotes Psalms 37:24: *Though he fall, he shall not be utterly cast down, for the Lord upholds him with his hand.*

Later, I began to be concerned about my finances. I

thought, how crazy it was to get rid of that amount of money when I don't even know how much I may need for a nursing home or health expenses. The next moment, God said to me, "Daddy Warbucks." When this message registered, I laughed and laughed. In the cartoon, "Orphan Annie," Daddy War bucks was always the one who arrived in the nick of time with his army of bodyguards to rescue Annie from any dilemma: physical, emotional or *financial!* Then I knew God was telling me that he is my Daddy Warbucks and I have nothing to fear. Praise God: my Helper, my Rescuer, my Adviser, my Savior.

One morning I was showing a friend through the Lighthouse Rescue Mission when we found an old man sitting on a bed. Jim was a tall, lean cowboy-type with a rugged outdoor face. The boots beside his bed were run down, worn out and full of holes. He hadn't been on a horse lately, but he had been on the road for years, drifting from mission to mission, from Salvation Army soup kitchens to church basement sleeping rooms. But that day he appeared to be in pain. I asked him if he were ill, and he said that he was suffering from an untreated hernia. He had gone to the free medical clinic, but they told him they couldn't do surgery.

Immediately I called one of the surgeons in our church, asking if he would examine Jim. God must have spoken to Dr. Morris, for he told me to bring Jim to his office. That afternoon the surgeon called me out of the waiting room, telling me Jim had a strangulated hernia, and he would operate at once.

Anna came to the hospital room, and we both held the hands of a trembling, frightened cowboy, praying with him and for him while he waited for the gurney. The operation was quick and successful; Jim healed fast and he was in church the following Sunday.

With the help of dedicated Christian doctors, dentists, surgeons, ministers, counsellors and barbers, the Lighthouse has been able not only to feed and house the homeless, but also to give them necessary medical and dental help and advice on grooming and how to apply for a job. A lot of success stories have come from that once cold and empty warehouse.

The night after Anna and I had gotten Jim through the surgery successfully, the Holy Spirit was powerfully present in my bedroom. I awakened in the middle of the night with a light shining in my face. There was no spotlight or flashlight, no visible source of the light; I just realized there was a bright light completely surrounding me and *in me.* As Jesus said, *"If then your whole body is full of light, having no dark part, the whole body will be full of light, as when the bright shining of a lamp gives you light"* (Lk 11:36).

I then became aware of a hushed silence, a silence as profound as the 300 trumpets of Gideon about to sound, a silence so powerful that I shook in awe and wonder at what might come next. When I next looked into the room, almost the entire room was filled with a heavy fog or smoke, and its shape was of *a giant chariot.* I saw no details of the chariot, but the outside of it was sharp and definite, and its size was enormous, taking up a large portion of the master bedroom. To the side of the chariot was a sparkling human-shaped figure moving around. At that point, I felt fear, and the whole scene vanished.

What an awesome visitation! Perhaps the chariot was present to take me for a short visit with the Lord Jesus but I was too frightened to get out of bed and climb aboard. How can I doubt the Lord of the Universe is present with me all the time?

A few weeks ago the Lord sent the hymn "Soon, very soon, I'm going to see the Lord." All day. So I wondered if he would show himself as he did in November 1988 (a visitation described in my book *These Last Days).* So I looked at people all day to see if anyone looked like Jesus. One stranger, a released prisoner, came in the Lighthouse and was about the right size, but I don't remember his face. Lord, if it was you, forgive me. I simply wasn't thinking about you when he came in.

Two other times after Howard died I have wakened in the night with a message from the Holy Spirit that Jesus was coming to see me. Then I have heard footsteps coming down the hallway. Immediately, I said, "Please no, Lord, I can't handle seeing a man at my bedroom door in the middle of a dark night." I am embarrassed and ashamed of my cowardice, but weakness and fear are common reactions to a powerful spiritual presence. Daniel felt this too: *"Therefore I was left alone when I saw this great vision, and no strength remained in me ..."* (10:8). St. John on Patmos said, *And when I saw him, I fell at his feet as dead. But he laid his right hand on me, saying to me, "Do not be afraid; I am the First and the Last"* (Rev 1:17). One day, I hope to be ready to see the Lord face to face. Lord, help me not to fear.

Not only has the Lord Jesus come at night and I was too frightened to see him, but one night it was an angel, I feel certain. I wakened at 1:15 a.m. and watched a shadow pass across the clock. Angels, I thought! Then I heard a ka-lump, ka-lump, ka-lump coming down the hallway. I was in the Spirit and knew it was in the spiritual realm. I was frightened and started coming out of the Spirit. Immediately, the sound stopped, and everything withdrew. My bones are so filled with the clay of the earth that God is going to have a hard time elevating me into higher truths.

One evening a neighbor who visited often and had become a close friend took me to a pizza parlor for supper since his wife was out of town that day. We laughed and talked, as usual, and both enjoyed it. But the Lord was not pleased. In the night he sent a vision of a huge eye and ear. Then he said the word, "Perception" to my consciousness. I then understood it was the perception of evil I should avoid. Accompanying that was his absence all night. I really knew I had goofed.

"Choose the narrow gate" was the message that came to me when the finance committee, of which I was a member, scheduled an important budget meeting on a Sunday afternoon. I had been trying to follow the Lord's admonition concerning the keeping of the Sabbath: *"If you turn away your foot from the Sabbath, from doing your pleasure on my holy day, and call the Sabbath a delight, the holy day of the Lord honorable, and shall honor him, not doing your own ways, nor finding your own pleasure, nor speaking your own words, then you shall delight yourself in the Lord; and I will cause you to ride on the high hills of the earth, and feed you with the heritage of Jacob your father. The mouth of the Lord has spoken"* (Isa 58:13,14). Jesus himself did not cancel the commandment to keep the Sabbath holy. He was simply opposed to the legalistic way the temple authorities broke the spirit of the law in keeping the letter of the law.

That afternoon, instead of going to the finance meeting, I attended a concert of Handel's "Messiah." As I sat in the auditorium, listening to the strains of that great oratorio roll over my head, hearing the heart of the composer break with Christ's betrayal and rejoice with his victory over death, a message impressed itself on my consciousness, "For the want of a nail, a shoe was lost; for the want of a shoe, a horse was lost ..."

"What?" I thought. "God, why are you sending me this message right now in the middle of a beautiful concert?" It was weeks later when I realized that the horse-shoe-nail message was sent by the evil one to try to ruin the concert for me by making me feel uneasy and guilty about missing the meeting. I won that battle, but have lost several others.

Our town's large new community center is a masterpiece of architecture and acoustics. All kinds of programs, concerts and plays are scheduled for performance before the citizens of the community. In the past I have attended them as often as my schedule permitted. However, the Lord sent a very vivid dream to explain what was really happening to me when I chose to attend some of them.

In the dream, I was at the theater seeing a play or program of some kind that included music and dancing. When it was over, I went backstage to deliver a package to someone. While walking, I became aware of tracking through mud, and it was all over my shoes. The thought came as I continued the errand that I could wade through puddles of water on the sidewalk to clean off the mud. I did and much of the mud came off, but not all. There was still a little mud on my shoes. Dear God, it is *still* there! When we participate in the world, the world sticks to us. It is like taffy on one's hands. We try to rub it off, and it gets all over the other hand. Secular things are not for me, the Lord says. I need to have all the mud off of my shoes to receive God's messages and deliver them to others.

As though to confirm this, God sent another vision in which I saw the sparkling jewels of heaven, but on top of them flowed a film of mud and trash. Their sparkle and beauty was covered by an ugly brown stain. The Lord seemed to be saying that I was allowing the world to intrude too much, so the jewels of truth and beauty couldn't shine through my life. I knew then that God wanted to keep me on a short chain and I needed to be thankful for this.

Another dream followed soon afterward reinforcing this conclusion. I was driving my car in a field or pasture, but saw in the distance a highway I was trying to get to. Every time I approached the highway, a deep rut or a huge downed tree or a steep embankment prevented me from driving up onto the highway. I woke up in frustration. The explanation came to me the next morning. I can see myself being completely in God's will for me, and visualize it, and want it, but something is always in the way. Lord, have mercy. This is getting deep.

In contrast to some of the purely secular programs I was exposed to at the community center, one Christmas a friend invited me to see an original musical pageant at St. Luke's Episcopal Church called "People of the Inn" by Deloris McCreary. It was a wonderful story of ordinary people who were staying at the Bethlehem Inn and how they were changed by the Baby Jesus being born in a stable behind the inn. The music was excellent, the setting was believable and an empty space in a widow's heart was filled with wonder and joy that evening.

After returning home, I began to wonder why God would want his Son to be born in such a crude place as a barn with animals present. I thought back on life in a common inn and how many lies were probably told within its walls, how many thefts, murders, violent words or actions may have occurred there. I also thought about the spirits of these evil deeds that might still be present inside the walls of that inn, like the mud on my shoes from being where I shouldn't be. Then I realized a baby would be safer in the presence of the gentle spirits of sheep, cattle and donkeys – servant spirits to bless God's Servant Son and man's Servant King.

We are all called to be servants of each other. One morning I woke with the Philippian scripture running through my head: *Let this mind be in you which was also in Christ Jesus, who, being in the form of God, did not consider it robbery to be equal with God, but made himself of no reputation, taking the form of a servant ...* (2:5-7). I wondered all day what God was trying to say to me. That afternoon my friend Miriam asked if I would help her deliver calendars to retired school teachers all over town. This took two hours. Instead of grinding my teeth at having to postpone some important things I wanted to do, I remembered the morning' scripture and rejoiced at the opportunity to be a servant to someone. This is a lesson I need help remembering.

Many times God warns me of approaching traffic problems or various kinds of dangers. One afternoon he sent an old secular song with the line, "Keep your hand upon the throttle and your eye upon the rail." He has reminded me of this song many times when I was about to encounter a verbal conflict with someone, but that particular day, I was supposed to take it literally.

As I hurried out to the nursing home to lead gospel singing, I glanced at the speedometer and noticed I was going over 45 mph in a 40 mph zone. I slowed down just before reaching a parked city patrolman with a radar gun set to check speeds of approaching vehicles. God is more interested in mercy than strict justice and I thanked him for saving me from a traffic ticket. Micah says of God, *He has shown you, O man, what is good; and what does the Lord require of you but to do justly, to love mercy, and to walk humbly with your God?* (6:8).

Another warning I remember receiving was hearing the words "Be careful with breakfast" as I wakened. It was summer in Oklahoma and very hot. As I reached in the refrigerator for milk for breakfast, I realized the bottle I had purchased the day before was still in the trunk of my very hot car and had been there since yesterday afternoon. So down the sink it went. There seemed to be a tablespoon of milk left in the old bottle so I prayed over it, then poured it over a serving of cold cereal. It kept pouring and pouring out of the bottle until there was plenty of milk to wet the cereal, plus a tablespoon left in the bottom of the bowl after I had eaten the cereal. How good God is! This kind of miracle is available to everyone who believes in miracles, loves God, trusts God and humbly asks.

One morning I wakened to a beautiful vision of my own bathroom. It was clean and shiny. The pink lavatory and counter top were polished, every item on it neat and orderly. The floral wallpaper looked especially beautiful against the carpet. I hurried to the bathroom and surveyed the real thing and realized it was not picture perfect, so that morning I cleaned it carefully. A week later the Lord sent a vision of my garage—tidied and in order. I followed suit and cleaned the garage that day, but when I was finished, neither of them looked as pretty as the visions.

I kept wondering what was the purpose of the visions. God has a reason for every message. While I pondered this, the Lord said to my inner being, "Be perfect for I am perfect," (paraphrased from Jesus' Sermon on the Mount–Mt 6:48). I understood then that I am to follow his guidance in *every* thought, act, attitude and motive. It sounds like a simple assignment, but it is incredibly difficult. I need God's constant help to observe this stricture.

I still remember the lesson the Lord sent one day by way of a tiny hummingbird. He flew into my screened-in porch through the door I had propped open for the rug cleaners who were coming. He was flying around the porch, frantically looking for the door. I tried to shoo him in the right direction, but he wouldn't go. Finally I brought a ladder and with a fly swatter gently guided him into a corner, climbed the ladder and reached up to where he was, cupping him in both hands. He was very still and made no noise at all. He weighed practically nothing, and I paused to marvel at the distance hummingbirds migrate every year. Then I took him outside and opened both hands. When he noticed he was not bound, he flew away straight toward the trees. I murmured a little blessing, wished him safe passage and felt my eyes moisten with the tenderness.

I thought how God must grieve when we get ourselves caught in difficult situations. He tries to guide us gently back to the path, but in our stubbornness, we insist on our own way of self- destruction. Sometimes his hand has to take us forcibly away from traps we have entered by allowing natural consequences to follow. Then when we call upon him for help, asking forgiveness for our sins, he opens his hand and releases us—with blessings and with tears. We only have to accept it and fly to safety. Praise God, our Redeemer.

9

The Serpent

Whenever I waken in the middle of the night, hearing a hideous groan that seems to be half-human, half-animal, I know the evil one has gotten into the house again. So I start searching my life during the past few days for what I have thought, done, or allowed in the house. Sometimes it is as simple as watching news of violence on television, listening to gossip, being envious or resentful of someone, failing to fulfill a commitment, or not being totally obedient to God's personal instructions.

I have learned that Lucifer can and does read minds, can throw in thoughts and words, even in the midst of a communication from God to confuse God's message, can disguise himself as God so cleverly as to deceive even the saints. Jesus said, *"For false Christs and false prophets will arise and show great signs and wonders, so as to deceive, if possible, even the elect"* (Mt 24:24).

The evil one's intention is not only to destroy physical life and health, but also our faith and trust in God, our spiritual well-being, our sanity, our reputations and our influence. To prevent this, our defenses must be sure, our guard up and our prayer life full.

> *Finally, my brethren, be strong in the Lord and in the power of his might. Put on the whole armor of God, that you may be able to stand against the wiles of the devil. For we do not wrestle against flesh and blood, but against principalities, against powers, against the rulers of the darkness of this age, against spiritual hosts of wickedness in the heavenly places. Therefore, take up the whole armor of God, that you may be able to withstand in the evil day, and having done all, to stand.*
>
> *Stand therefore, having girded your waist with truth, having put on the breast-plate of righteousness, and having shod your feet with the preparation of the gospel of peace; above all, taking the shield of faith with which you will be able to quench all the fiery darts of the wicked one. And take the helmet of salvation, and the sword of the Spirit, which is the Word of God* (Eph 6:10-17).

The above conclusions have been drawn through sometimes bitter, embarrassing, and painful experiences. Most of them can be confirmed by similar incidents in the Bible. I have had many personal experiences that illustrate how the serpent works.

I used to think it would be easier to live a holy life and be fully obedient to the Lord as time passed. But no! The more progress we make toward the kingdom, the more barbs come toward us from the serpent. The Bible calls him Lucifer because he once appeared as an angel of light or son of the morning.

> *How you are fallen from heaven, O Lucifer, son of the morning! How you are cut down to the ground, you who weakened the nations! For you have said in your heart: "I will ascend into heaven, I will exalt my throne above the stars of God; I will also sit on the mount of the congregation on the farthest sides of the north; I will ascend above the heights of the clouds, I will be like the Most High." Yet you shall be brought down to Sheol, to*

the lowest depths of the Pit (Isa 14:12-15).

The first time I became aware of a direct action toward me by the evil force on our planet, I was terrified. Howard and I had passed some cross words over something minor. In the night I awakened to a vision of brown specks moving around in some green slime. It was hideous and made me nauseous. Immediately, I started calling out, "Jesus, Jesus, Jesus, praise him." The ugly scene disappeared and was replaced by sparkling jewels of heaven. The next day I anointed the whole house and there was peace and lightness all day.

Since then, interference has become a regular occurrence and I have learned the extent to which the evil one will go to distort, confuse, or destroy God's message. Yes, God is sovereign, but people have chosen not to obey God, instead to be their own gods. Thus, we have chosen to be obedient to the elemental forces of the universe and be subject to our own physical desires and drives. Most people do not realize the power we are giving to the enemies of God in the process.

Many times the Lord has started sending a vision of beautiful heavenly scenes: roses, lilies, golden objects that have been intricately patterned or a screen of beautiful colors. The next thing I would see was a black inkblot forming over the most beautiful part or a splash of yellowish-brown slop running down across the screen. Sometimes the intrusion consists of demon monsters with bared teeth and ugly yellow eyes. They look like the faces of toy monsters the children next door play with, but these night-intruders are live spiritual monsters, and they seem to be trying to get into my eyes. I have learned to call out the name "*Jesus*" repeatedly to rid the room and the vision of evil intruders. But in the process the entire vision disappears and I am out of the Spirit.

When I no longer was able to associate their presence with

some identifiable sin in my life, I decided the evil forces in the world are advancing and multiplying at a tremendous rate as a prelude to the millennium when the Lord Jesus will come and the demons will be chained and banished for a thousand years (Rev 20:1-3).

After repeated questioning of the Lord as to why I was being attacked so fiercely and how to prevent it, the Lord sent an unmistakable message. Someone shook me awake one night, but when I looked up, nobody was there. Immediately, I knew I was in the Spirit for my vision was grainy and pebbly. I heard the far-off din of voices and songs coming across the veil of eternity and my body was gripped by a powerful electric force. I looked at the wall where pictures are usually sent and saw nothing. Then I drifted back to sleep. Someone took hold of my shoulder and wakened me again. This time the Lord started sending a vision of windows – many, many windows. That disappeared and I saw a dam with water spilling over. Into my mind was placed the realization that the dam was my bedroom door sill to the outside porch where light came in under draperies that were too short. Then I remembered a dream in which I went about a house closing windows and checking doors before going upstairs to bed. I found I had left the upstairs bedroom window open and it was raining in on the bed.

All this activity was to prepare me to understand the command to close off doors, windows and outside light to the bedroom or else demons would dance on my bed every night as a distraction from receiving messages from God. I was to close off my bedroom in the same manner Moses did when he made curtains for the Holy of Holies in the ancient tabernacle (Ex 26). I knew from this that we are in a serious business in this latter part of the 20th century.

So I anointed the whole house and covered up the opening under the drapery to the sliding glass door. There was peace all night. The Lord sent a vision of stars in the dark night, and through them wove a cloud of lighted fog. I thought it might be the Holy Spirit patrolling the entire universe. There was no interference from the evil one in anything.

The next night, however, was an entirely different story. I wakened in the middle of the night to a loud hideous groan. I sprang awake and ordered evil out. Then I remembered watching television news showing violence and bloodshed. *That* opened a gateway for evil to come into the house.

The Scripture which most nearly explains this closing off of all dressing and sleeping rooms is in Ezekiel: *And the galleries all around their three stories opposite the threshold were paneled with wood from the ground to the windows—the windows were covered ...* (41:16). Ezekiel was shown in a vision how the children of Israel were to rebuild the temple when they returned from the Babylonian captivity. The instructions were to cover the windows of the rooms where the priests changed clothing. The naked body was not to be exposed to the demons of the air, else the bodies of the priests of the Most High God could be invaded and distracted from their ministry, leading the people astray.

Once I wakened late at night to see three cats on my bed. I screamed, "Jesus, Jesus," and they disappeared. Once it was brown rats; twice it was a brown recluse spider walking across my arm; once it was a huge black tarantula spider in a rope-like web next to my face; many times, it was horrible demon-like dragons or huge reptiles with yellow eyes and huge sharp teeth trying to climb into my eyes or scream in my ears with half-human, half-animal howls. Sometimes the intrusion late at night consisted of the sound of a powerful explosion right outside my window. I would waken with a start, but realize immediately that it was in the spiritual, not physical, dimension. The explosions might have been battles between warring angels and evil spirits just outside my bedroom. The unmistakable truth is the evil forces of the universe want to stop people who are working for the Lord.

Paul the Apostle reports being hassled by demons repeatedly: *And lest I should be exalted above measure by the abundance of the revelations, a thorn in the flesh was given to me, a messenger of Satan to buffet me, lest I be exalted above measure* (2 Cor 12:7). Also: *Therefore we wanted to come to you—even I, Paul, time and again—but Satan hindered us* (1 Thess 2:18).

Jesus makes a number of references to Satan, devils or demons, including his temptation in the wilderness by Satan, the head of that army of evil angels whom also he defeated at Calvary. Thus 1 John tells us, *He who sins is of the devil, for the devil has sinned from the beginning. For this purpose the Son of God was manifested, that he might destroy the works of the devil* (3:8).

An amazing confirmation of demons hassling people has come from a fascinating book, *Send Me your Guardian Angel, Padre Pio,* by Fr. Alessio Parente. Padre Pio was a 19th century Italian monk who was extremely sensitive to the spirit world. He reported the evil one intruding on and trying to destroy his legitimate visions from God, just as I have experienced. Also he was so severely attacked by demons at night that he frequently asked friends to sit by his bedside all night to pray for him.

I did not wish to include a long discourse about demons in this book, but I feel that it is needed, especially in today's society as a warning against the horrors this subtle evil being is capable of initiating.

One morning when I was in the midst of breakfast, a voice came to me saying, "We have mice that will cut off your power!" The voice was gloating and sarcastic, and I knew immediately who it was. Then I remembered hearing noises in the wall of my utility room. So it was mice in the wall and they could gnaw through the insulation on the electric lines, starting a fire. "Lord, what shall I do?" I pleaded. On the way to morning prayer, I switched on the radio to hear a minister quote *"Not by might, nor by power, but by my spirit," says the Lord of Hosts* (Zech 4:6b).

"Thank you, Lord," I said, for I knew then what to do. Upon returning home, I inspected the exterior of the house foot by foot to discover their entryway. The only opening I could find was a small space around the electric dryer outlet from the utility room. I then ordered out of the house all evil including mice, using the name of *Jesus,* to which every knee must bow, honor and obey (Phil 2:9-11). I waited until afternoon to allow the mice time to leave, then used cement mix with water to plaster the small opening around the dryer outlet. No further sound emanated from the wall. Thank God for his advice and care.

At times Satan takes a legitimate message from God, distorts it and sends it over and over again until complete confusion reigns over what God actually said. One two-week period, I kept hearing the Scripture verse from Luke in which Jesus said, *"But why do you call me 'Lord, Lord,' and do not do the things I say?"* (6:46). I also saw visions of blood vessels clogged with fat, followed by very dim jewels of heaven. Satan cannot duplicate God's brightness. The Lord had actually asked me that question when I was eating too much fast-food with french-fries and sausage pizzas. My eating habits improved immediately, but this accusatory verse kept ringing in my ears. I became convinced it was instigated by the evil one, until I drove it off by praise to God in songs and hymns.

Another incident of Satan sending a song of accusation to my consciousness were the lines "Why from the sunshine of life wilt thou roam farther and farther away?" from "Jesus is Tenderly Calling." The tune persisted time after time while I searched my being for the dreadful thing I must have done to deserve this chastisement. Then it came to me that the worry and guilt I was experiencing were not of God. If I had an unconfessed sin, the Holy Spirit would bring it to my attention and I would acknowledge it, ask forgiveness and receive God's peace. But God would not continue to plague me with a reminder of that sin. The only one who would do that is Satan. The epistle to the Romans tells us: *There is therefore now no condemnation to those who are in Christ Jesus, who do not walk according to the flesh, but according to the Spirit* (8:1).

Many times Satan has threatened me with death in visions, in words and in physical events. My house on the hill sits five miles from town, and it used to be that on nearly every trip to town I managed to meet cars at the most dangerous location along the route, the railroad crossing. There are two sharp turns at the crossing of this narrow road and the tracks and it is blinding to meet a car there at night. Finally I rebuked Satan in Jesus' name and asked God's protection. Now I seldom meet another vehicle at the tracks, even in the daytime.

Our church youth held a Halloween concert of Christian music in the community center. Part of the music was rock music that is called "Christian Rock." The organizers asked our church prayer warriors to sit backstage and pray through the entire concert. We sat in a room behind the stage, prayed and read Scripture aloud for three hours. Some of the music that seeped through the wall was soft, melodic and tender; but the rock music, even though the word "Jesus" graced the words, resounded loud and heavy. It had a driving beat that was erotic and it seemed to me its source was the devil.

If we compromise with the devil, he will have us for breakfast. Though I spoke a warning to the sponsors of the event telling them such rock music did not seem to me of the Lord, my words were not well received. However, the word I heard from the Lord was to stand the ground he gave me and keep my forehead hard as flint.

Satan often tries to intercept God's messages and distort them. Four months before Howard died, a word came from the Lord that he planned to take Howard soon. God had told me in the past that he would tell me things to come. As Jesus said, *"When he, the Spirit of truth, has come, he will guide you into all truth; for he will not speak on his own authority, but whatever he hears he will speak, and he will tell you things to come"* (Jn 16:13).

In the midst of the powerful sweeping Spirit of God touching me and delivering this message, another voice added, "before Christmas." Immediately I rejected the entire communication because I didn't know Satan could superimpose words on top of God's voice. I thought the whole utterance came from the evil one.

In the same way, Satan has brought many lying messages to confuse me. On a weekend I planned to visit my family in Missouri, I wakened with the words "Don't go today" in my ears. It did not sound as though it were of the Lord. Immediately the Lord sent a vision of a checkered winner flag distorted so the whites were together and the blacks together instead of black against white. This was the Lord's way of showing me that the preceding message was false. I did go to Missouri that weekend and had a great trip.

At that point, to dissuade me from following God's orders, Satan began sending visions of a checkered winner flag whenever I started to do anything important. I have become convinced that Satan has assigned numbers of demons to follow us around throwing obstacles in our paths. I am trying to learn to laugh at him, for I know he cannot do anything to harm me, and he cannot stand to be laughed at. Also I must learn to rely on inner witness, the still, small voice of God which cannot be duplicated, to determine who is speaking to my spirit.

One snowy night I traveled to Tulsa to see the Arthur Miller play "The Crucible" set to music. It is the story of the Salem witch-hunt that occurred during the early days of America. While riding to Tulsa on the opera bus through the falling flakes of snow, I thought about the warnings God had given me about participating in evil by watching it.

I suspected that I really should not go to see this musical, for when I had asked the Lord about it, he directed me to two passages in Isaiah: [God said], *"This is the way; walk ye in it"* (30:21), and then the description of one who pleases the Lord as *"He who walks righteously and speaks uprightly, he who despises the gain of oppressions, who gestures with his hands, refusing bribes, who stops his ears from hearing of bloodshed, and shuts his eyes from seeing evil"* (33:15).

The opera did depict satanic activity by some young girls of the Salem colony, culminating in evil and dreadful injustice. At one point, pins and needles were thrust into a rag doll or puppet, and one of the characters was cursed, later to be falsely accused and executed by hanging. It was supposed to be a true story and if so there was a great miscarriage of justice.

All the way home I had a foreboding of evil, but didn't know until later that night how much evil I had brought home by viewing that play. In the night I wakened to a frightening vision of a huge spider web with strands the size of ropes. On it crept an enormous black spider that looked like a giant tarantula the size of a pint jar. The spider was trying to crawl into my eye. I sang out "Jesus, Jesus" several times, and the vision faded. I ordered evil out in the name of Jesus and asked forgiveness for going to the opera, but every time I closed my eyes, there was the ugly vision.

It hung on tenaciously, strengthening whenever I stopped saying the name of *Jesus.* I finally turned on the light, arose from bed and washed my face to become thoroughly awake, walked over the entire house pleading the blood of Jesus on myself, the house and contents. I was able to return to sleep an hour or so later and had no more trouble that night.

But I had not completely dispelled the evil from the house and from me. There was still mud on my shoes. The next night I was roused from sleep to receive a vision of pins and needles dropping through the air, sent by the evil one. This was to remind me of the section in the opera where young girls were sticking pins in puppets to inflict evil on other people. It was as though the evil one were saying, "Aha, you see what I can do to you." I rose from bed and repeated the cleansing and sanctifying I had done the night before. It took about a week to rid the house of the evil spirits I had brought home because of seeing that play.

I have been told that hard-core pornography is not only viewing pictures of sexual acts but also watching real murders in pictures or on video. If that is true, news pictures of war scenes in which people are being wounded and killed are also pornography. That was confirmed to me one night after I watched a news clip of the Bosnian conflict.

That night I received an attack from the evil forces of the planet. I wakened to a scene pressing itself on me as a vision. First I saw many eyes forming on a plain screen. They seemed to be evil for they were trying to bore into my head, and I felt the evil on myself as they forced themselves on me. I immediately started calling the name, "Jesus, Jesus, Jesus!" I opened my eyes and saw a spiritual black cat spring from my bed and dart out the bedroom door. I got up, washed my face and started praying. I asked forgiveness for my sins, claimed the blood of Jesus covering me and slept peacefully the rest of the night.

But Satan's most serious breach of my defenses occurred in

1994. Someone, whom I thought to be the Lord, warned me of a coming fierce winter. The visions sent were of high snowfalls, ice storms that would cause power lines to break, leaving people who were particularly vulnerable without heat, food or medicine. Every week, reminders would cross my consciousness that I must warn people to prepare for bad weather. When I consulted the Bible, it would open on passages containing the word "snow," or warnings by various prophets of coming disasters. Even when I was quietly listening to cassette tapes of Scripture and closed my eyes to listen better, a vision was sent to my spiritual eyes of a snow scene or a storm.

I finally decided to warn people through a letter to the editor of our local newspaper. But a bad storm did not arrive. We experienced a few thin snows and a touch of ice, but the big one I was expecting never occurred.

Kind friends said the Lord relented at the prayers of the town citizens. Others said Jonah was allowed to preach destruction advancing on Nineveh, and it didn't happen because the people of Nineveh repented. But I am forced to recognize that I swallowed the bait Satan dangled in front of me and took a hook along with it. Satan's plan was to destroy my reputation as a prophet and cause me to be ridiculed, laughed at, mocked and discredited, especially when I speak the Lord's words of warning about the approaching close of the age when Jesus returns, the church is raptured and terrible tribulation arises for those who are left on this planet.

The Lord sent a dream to illustrate his reaction to that prophecy which was not fulfilled. I was upstairs in a bathroom getting ready to take a shower when I noticed a water pipe leaking. Much water was present on the pipe junction and flowing down the pipe, but it seemed to disappear before getting the floor wet. Nevertheless I felt the need to have it repaired, so I rushed downstairs where I found my own earthly father, who has been dead 50 years, carrying a large pipe wrench. He said he would come upstairs and fix it. In the meantime, all my friends and acquaintances were trudging upstairs, filing through my bathroom, exclaiming over the water leak. At that point, I felt their disapproval and condemnation. Then I wakened.

When I told this story to a pastor friend, she roared with laughter and said, "Many people think you have a leak." At that I joined in the laughter. She added, "If something is seriously wrong in your life, your Heavenly Father will fix it." How comforting!

The Lord also sent a comforting hymn to my consciousness, "The Strife is Over, the Battle Done." The first line continues, "the victory of life is won; the song of triumph has begun; Alleluia! The powers of death have done their worst, but Christ their legions hath dispersed; let shouts of holy joy outburst, Alleluia." It is a hymn of triumph. So God is not going to let me go. I have asked forgiveness for my pride or whatever sin I have been living in and feel assured I am forgiven. Praise God!

To further uplift me, God reminded me that Job was hassled severely by Satan but God restored double what Job had lost. As a way to emphasize his forgiveness of my sin of listening to the devil and mistaking the message, he sent a glorious vision on my bedroom wall that night. God wakened me and I was in the Spirit. On the bedroom wall I saw the glory of God in the form of light without a source. In the middle of the light was a beautiful multicolored fluttering butterfly. It didn't look like a picture on the wall, but an actual butterfly in the room. After a short time the whole vision faded. The message I heard was that God does not condemn us for failing. Praise the Lord!

10

Angels

Since I first saw the military angels in my backyard several years ago, I have been aware of the presence of some kind of angels almost continually. The circumstance of their first presence was told in detail in my book *These Last Days.*

They were seven or eight feet tall, dressed in tunics like ancient Roman soldiers, wearing helmets with spikes on top and capes suspended from their shoulders. The entire frame of one who was obviously their leader was illuminated from within and behind his body with constantly moving lights which changed from red to white to purple to gold in varying intensities. Luke describes the angels who rolled the stone away from Jesus' tomb thus: *And it happened, as they were greatly perplexed about this, that behold, two men stood by them in shining garments* (24:4).

The figures I saw appeared slightly foggy, indistinct and translucent. At the time, their leader Michael told me they were guarding me from the evil one. I was deeply in the Spirit when I saw them. One cannot see into the spiritual realm except through spiritual eyes. Perhaps it would be well to tell here how I received the gift of being "in the Spirit."

The Curtis Hooper painting of Jesus, which was modeled on the Shroud of Turin image, was published in *Life* magazine in February 1982. Later I came across this picture and studied it intently. I set it across the room from where I was ironing and week after week looked at the pained, tortured face of the crucified man who was called Savior of the world. I wept part of the time as I thought of his suffering; I talked to him as though he were in the room; I sang praises to him for his eternal goodness and mercy.

One day, in my eyes, I saw his face lose the tortured appearance and take on an expression of deep love. I was so delighted and overwhelmed that Jesus would allow me to see *himself* I could hardly contain my excitement. From that moment, I knew what it meant to see with spiritual eyes. The face itself in the painting had not changed, but my eyes were seeing the Spiritual Jesus. The gift was given because of my deep and intense worship of the Savior. It was a short step from there into speaking "in tongues," hearing sounds from heaven and participating in several other of the nine spiritual gifts:

> *Now concerning spiritual gifts, brethren, I do not want you to be ignorant; ... Now there are diversities of gifts, but the same Spirit. There are differences of ministries, but the same Lord ... for to one is given the word of wisdom through the Spirit, to another the word of knowledge through the same Spirit, to another faith by the same Spirit, to another gifts of healings by the same Spirit, to another the working of miracles, to another prophecy, to another discerning of spirits, to another different kinds of tongues, to another the interpretation of tongues. But one and the same Spirit works all these things, distributing to each one individually as he wills* (1 Cor 12:1-11).

Since seeing the large military angels several years ago, I have come to realize angels exist in a wide variety of sizes and shapes. Some have wings and some don't. More than once I have wakened in the Spirit in the middle of the night to see an ordinary looking man standing beside my bed. The appearance lasted only until I registered in my mind that *someone* was in the room, then it vanished.

Sometimes the night visitor appears as a woman. One night I was listening off and on to the Gospel of John being played on a tape recorder at my bedside table. I dozed at times, but when I opened my eyes I saw a woman dressed in a white robe floating above my head with her arm outstretched and her hand pointing toward the tape recorder. She was a beautiful blond woman, appearing to be 20 or 30 years old, but as soon as I saw her, she disappeared. She had no wings attached to her body.

Another time, I wakened to see either the same or a similar woman in a robe sitting beside the bed, looking at me and smiling. One night she was standing beside the bed with her right hand on my head and her left hand upraised. During an afternoon nap, I opened my eyes to see a woman in a pink robe hovering over me with her hand raised in a blessing. One night the visitor was a man in white trousers and shirt, also with one hand on my head and the other upraised.

Often in the middle of the night, I have been aware of a fluttering sound, then a thump, as though someone with wings had flown in and landed on the floor beside the bed. Sometimes the landing is on the bed itself, then the whole bed shakes. I must admit to being a little unnerved when this happens.

One night the Lord allowed me to see a portion of an angel wing in sharp detail. It was very large, taking up most of the distance between floor and ceiling of the bedroom. I seemed to be seeing it from the underside. The inner structure was a little like a butterfly wing with struts and braces visible under a very thin covering with the appearance of finest batiste. The color was pale green. For the briefest moment I saw this wing portion long enough to examine it and store it in my memory. I did not see the creature to which the wing was attached.

Last fall I wakened to see a red light on my bedside table. A flutter of wings moved toward me and a round face appeared in my vision. The face was heavily bearded with light reddish-brown hair and was abnormally round. The eyes shone bright and smiling, but the face drew so near my face, I began to be alarmed. The vision disappeared. The creature attached to the wings and bearded face could not have been more than eight-inches tall.

After spending the evening singing through an old hymnal, thinking about Jesus and worshiping him, I wakened in the night to see a mass of green fog in front of my face. I could make out eyes and a mouth before it vanished. The whole ball of fog was only about eight inches in diameter. I am currently puzzling about the apparent absence of a *body* on these small angels or cherubs.

After Howard died, I became aware of the deep loneliness widows experience. Someone mentioned her husband warming her back at night and I realized that as being one thing I missed quite a lot. That very night the Lord sent two angels to sleep with me, one on either side. Somehow, in the middle of sleep, I realized there were two people in bed with me. I never reasoned why they were there or who they could be, just accepted their warmth and comfort. The next morning I rolled over, expecting to see somebody, and they were gone. Angels. *The angel of the Lord encamps around all those who fear him, and delivers them* (Ps 34:7). *Then as he [Elijah] lay and slept under a broom tree, suddenly an angel touched him, and said to him, "Arise and eat."* (1 Kings 19:5).

A few months after Howard's death, I wakened one morning, lay still for a few minutes, then heard a man's loud yawn beside me. I quickly looked over on the other side of the bed, but there was nobody, of course. Then I laughed and laughed, for the Holy Spirit was teasing me again. He had sent an angel to lie beside me to let me know I was not alone.

I awakened one night to see a man's hand and arm move across my face and upper body. I felt this blessing as a mild electrical shock moving from head to toe into every cell. I cried and rejoiced at this unexpected and undeserved blessing.

I have seen wavy lines and moving columns of fog in the bedroom almost every night. These angels are a tremendous comfort. I know I am being protected in every way when they are here. At times when an attack comes in the spiritual realm, I realize that angels are nearby so nothing can really harm me. If I have sinned in some manner, I quickly ask forgiveness and resolve to avoid getting into that situation again. Then I try to get back into the kingdom quickly.

One night when I had just gone to bed, the room flashed light and a heavy fog came to the side of the bed. I thrust my hand into it and my hand disappeared in the fog. At the same time I felt tingly and my whole body became hot. It felt as though someone had picked me up and held me to his breast. My face was pushed in a little as though it were pressed against someone's chest. I felt electrified and very hot. I thought I might be taken somewhere in the Spirit to talk to Jesus but was not. After a while–who knows how long–I found myself back on the bed. Was it angels or was it the Holy Spirit himself?

11

Theological Mysteries

I have recently become acquainted with a wonderful Full Gospel minister named Sarah Ann. Sarah is a little past retirement age, tall, strong and healthy, with steel-gray hair pulled back in a bun, piercing blue eyes and the voice of a master sergeant. She gets up in the morning with The Word and goes to bed at night with The Word. Scriptures and prayers pour out of her mouth like water over a dam. Her constant study, meditation and self-discipline have built up a huge reservoir of spiritual knowledge and blessings that overflows whenever and wherever needed. Sometimes the overflow comes as words of prophecy from the Lord.

I met her shortly after Howard died, and we have been fast friends ever since. When I have needed a word of chastisement from the Lord, she has not been hesitant to give it, and when I have needed comfort or advice from on high, she always knew how to bring that too. I have learned many theological truths under her teaching.

One day while speaking about the commandments of the Lord, Sarah said, "Obeying God's commandments includes not just the Ten Commandments, but whatever he asks us personally to accomplish." She added, "He never lightly commands anything. There are reasons for every command, *whether we know the reasons or not.* With God we always have free choices. It's the devil that tries to hem us in." She said we must be holy. Holiness, she added, goes along with love and faith. If we have one of the three, God supplies the other two. She said we must seek the face of Jesus. In some way, he will show us his face and his glory.

Sarah manifests two spiritual gifts that are not listed in the 1 Corinthians 12 passage. Those nine gifts, recorded by Paul, are the word of wisdom, word of knowledge, faith, healings, miracles, prophecy, discerning of spirits, tongues and interpretations. In addition to most of these, God has given Sarah *the gift of laughter and the gift of tears.*

The gift of laughter is becoming known around the United States and in parts of Canada in new Christian churches with names like The Church of Holy Laughter. The Spirit of the joy of the Lord and of salvation becomes so powerful in the hearts of people that the church congregation breaks out in gales of laughter. I have seen this phenomenon in small groups of people but not in a whole congregation. I have never experienced the gift of laughter, but I have experienced the gift of tears. At times when I have asked forgiveness for the nation because of the many abominations that were and are occurring almost daily, a wave of deep sorrow has passed over me, and I have wept without really understanding it.

There are scriptural confirmations for both of these phenomena. In Philippians Paul says, *"Rejoice in the Lord Always. Again I will say, rejoice"* (4:4). John tells us Jesus said, *"Therefore you now have sorrow; but I will see you again and your heart will rejoice and your joy no one will take from you"* (16:22). Also the Psalmist says: *When the Lord brought back the captivity of Zion, we were like those who dream. Then our mouth was filled with laughter, and our tongue with singing.* (126:1-2).

In John's gospel we find the single verse, *Jesus wept* (11:35). I've sometimes wondered why Jesus cried, because he certainly knew he was going to bring Lazarus back. After I saw Sarah on the floor once, curled up in the fetal position, emitting great heart-breaking sobs, I decided Jesus wept because he was feeling the deep sorrow of Mary and Martha at the death of their brother. His spirit was sensing and empathizing with their spirits in their sorrow. Sometimes this can happen in the Spirit without actually knowing why we are feeling so sorrowful.

One night I was strongly moved when I saw Sarah experiencing (in extreme) the gift of tears. One of the members of the congregation had told her how children are stripped of their self-confidence as they grow up in this culture. They are handicapped all of their lives because of a sense of inferiority. Sarah tried to start the worship service, then stopped and began to cry. Moans and audible weeping shook her body as she crouched on the floor by the altar rail. Her dear friend Marie sat beside her with a hand on her back, and I sat on the other side. But we could do nothing to lessen her grief.

As I sat there praying for her, it came to me that she was weeping over the sin which seems to blanket our nation and world: the aborted babies, sexual immorality, war and violence, people who turn away from God, the sin and moral degradation that are overtaking our civilization, the denial of Christ during the last two millennia, even the crucifixion of Jesus.

It is quite possible, even likely, that Jesus was the only one whose pain in dying was not partially alleviated by God. That is the only way it could have been the worst punishment anyone ever had, the only way that punishment would be great enough to cover the sins of all humankind for all time. And that pain was suffered by One who was totally innocent, yet totally in love with the people who were inflicting the pain.

Eventually when Sarah's weeping wore out, she rose and without comment conducted the service. She may not have known why she was crying, but God had sent the tears that needed to be shed and the anguish that needed to be felt over the world's sin.

To extend this observation, the Scripture talks about people who were once Christian, then backslide. *For if, after they have escaped the pollutions of the world through the knowledge of the Lord and Savior Jesus Christ, they are again entangled in them and overcome, the latter end is worse for them than the beginning. For it would have been better for them not to have known the way of righteousness, than having known it, to turn from the holy commandment delivered to them* (2 Pet 2:20-21).

Hebrews also talks about the effect a reversal of faith has on Jesus. *For it is impossible for those who were once enlightened, and have tasted the heavenly gift, and have become partakers of the Holy Spirit, and have tasted the good word of God and the powers of the age to come, if they fall away, to renew them again to repentance, since they crucify again for themselves the Son of God, and put him to an open shame* (6:4-6).

The Holy Spirit has entered and lived with the one who invites him in. So Jesus is intimately associated with the baptized Christian, and that person has partaken of the gifts of the Spirit. Thus regression and betrayal by the former confirmed Christian are devastating to the Holy Spirit. Jesus feels this betrayal, and he is crucified again in spirit. His grief is renewed.

The Stigmata is a mysterious phenomenon that has occurred many times since Jesus' day, particularly in the Roman

Catholic tradition. When the Spirit of Jesus is powerfully present in a sanctified person, especially at a time of innocent suffering, the Stigmata manifests itself as imprints on the body resembling marks of crucifixion. It is a sign of shared suffering with Jesus: *But rejoice to the extent that you partake of Christ's sufferings, that when his glory is revealed, you may also be glad with exceeding joy* (1 Pet 4:13).

With my own eyes, I saw the crucifixion mark on the palm of Miriam. She had placed her hand on the back of a man named Scott who had a history of back problems and pain. Several minutes of fervent prayer brought Spirit heat to her hand, accompanied by intense pain. The Spirit of God in the form of heat drained into Scott's hurting back. When the prayer was finished, Miriam's wrist had a deep indentation in it that was blood red, the Stigmata. And Scott, who had entered the chapel bent over from pain, walked out of the room upright and free.

We who witnessed this wonder were so much in awe that we didn't say a word, but each one of us knew we had seen a miracle, and it renewed our faith in the healing love of Jesus. The Stigmata on Miriam's wrist lasted several hours.

The workings of God in this universe is a mystery pondered by every thinker in the world, whether gifted theologian or lay person, math teacher or musician. What small child has watched the stars come out at night or pondered the Milky Way stretching from pole to pole and not wondered what it all means, and how they fit into God's plan? Does God's sovereignty stop where our human will begins?

I supposed God had a number of plans–Plan A, Plan B, Plan X according to how well people coöperate with his desires for their lives. I have also thought about God's reaching into the physical universe from time to time, changing his natural law to effect healings or miracles according to his sovereign will. I have even used the word "dabble" to indicate God's actions or reactions. But I was not really satisfied with those conclusions. One day while I was driving down the street contemplating this enigma, God seemed to say, *"I do not dabble!"*

Into my mind rolled an outline of the way God works. I do not know who sent this outline, but the gist of it is this: God is involved every second in sending the energy for every molecule to work. If he didn't, the universe would collapse. So God is presently and has for all time been sending energy into every molecule and every atom and every particle in the atom every moment–in every part of the universe. Also God is making a conscious *positive* decision concerning every particle of matter all the time.

What power and intellect God must possess to do that! I am continually in awe at the magnificence of a God who is intimately involved in the shade of coloring of the smallest flower, the aerodynamics of a hummingbird, or the intricate workings of a human eye, as well as the thought patterns of a mathematical genius or the musical perfection of a deaf Beethoven. And God blesses all this with his love, compassion, righteousness, justice and mercy.

God has not just spun the universe into motion and left it running on its own. God is the continuing power behind every particle of matter, energy, spirit–all the time. Jesus said, *"My Father has been working until now, and I am working"* (Jn 5:17).

So there is no Plan B. Since God knew before he created the world what decisions people would make concerning every matter and how he would respond to make the very best out of those decisions, all of God's plans are Plan A. *Peter, an apostle of Jesus Christ, to the pilgrims ... elect according to the foreknowledge of God the Father ...* (1 Pet 1:1-2).

For God to be a sovereign God, his Plan A is always in

effect and always good: *And we know that all things work together for good to those who love God, to those who are the called according to his purpose* (Rom 8:28).

Another theological mystery I have been pondering is the close connection between thoughts and physical reality. It is extremely important to think positive thoughts and speak positive words. Just as God speaks and it happens, we also can create the event with our words or thoughts. God has graciously given us this power. *"If you ask anything in my name, I will do it"* (Jn 14:14).

One day a friend called with a request for prayer for her daughter's marriage, which was about to end. Thinking about it in relation to the above principle, I recalled the story of the man who had terminal cancer and was healed when he visualized Jesus passing through his body destroying every bad cell. Then he praised God continuously day after day, hour after hour with joy and thanksgiving in his heart. After weeks of this visualization and praise, he got well. This man's name is Harry DeCamp, and he wrote his story in a little book called *One Man's Miracle* published by Guideposts.

I thought this could work in a marriage also, so I started visualizing Jesus in the home of this troubled couple, blessing them, causing each one to look at the other through Jesus' eyes, each one admitting Jesus into his/her heart and trying to please the other as though he or she were Jesus and each one forgiving the other for past hurts.

I kept up this prayer day after day. After a few weeks the crisis had ended and the family was together again – and still is. The Scriptural confirmation for this healing of a marriage is the simple command in Jesus' Sermon on the Mount: *"Ask, and it will be given you; seek, and you will find; knock, and it will be opened to you. For everyone who asks receives, and he who seeks finds, and to him who knocks, it will be opened"* (Mt 7:7-8).

Consider the mystery in the names of the first ten generations of people listed in Genesis. I heard a minister on the "Voice of Prophecy" say the first ten patriarchs of humanity were named by God to tell the story of human purpose on earth and the redemption of humanity by Jesus. Amazed at this idea, I immediately looked up in my Bible the names of our first ancestors and their meanings.

Adam means "man."
Seth means "appointed."
Enosh means "mortal."
Cainan means "fixed place or land."
Mahalaleel means "praise of God."
Jared means "descent."
Enoch means "dedicated."
Methuselah means "man of a javelin."
Lamech means "wild man."
Noah means "rest or comfort."

Therefore, if we were to make the meanings of these names into sentences, we would find: "Man was appointed as a mortal to the earth for the purpose of praising God. His Descendent was dedicated to elevating sinful man from disorder to peace."

It was an amazing coincidence – or was it – that I was studying the book of Isaiah on that particular day and read the passage: *"Since I appointed the ancient people. And the things that are coming and shall come ..."* (44:7).

We cannot doubt the existence of God and his intention at creation. If we coöperate with the Lord, receive the rest and comfort he sends through Jesus, lift our hearts and voices in God's praise, we will fulfill our purpose on earth. God told my friend Miriam that every sentence in the Bible contains layers upon layers of truth.

The mysteries in the story of the Ark of the Covenant are

myriad. God's instructions to Moses and to every generation since then came in the form of the Ten Commandments on stone tablets. The Ark of the Covenant which contained these stone tablets is now missing and, I expect, God intended it so. If someone ever found the Ark, it would henceforth become an object of worship like the Wailing Wall in Jerusalem.

When Jesus died on a cross almost 2,000 years ago, the veil of the temple was split in two from top to bottom, signifying no further need of the Holy of Holies, the most sacred place in the temple. The Holy Spirit of God from then on would live inside the hearts of the people of God, not in a house of wood, stone and fabric. And the Ark of the Covenant would no longer be needed to house the stone tablets of commandments to remind people of the laws of God. The Spirit of God himself would remind people from *inside them.*

In his Last Discourse Jesus told the disciples, *"And I will pray the Father, and he will give you another Helper, that he may abide with you forever, even the Spirit of truth, whom the world cannot receive, because it neither sees him nor knows him; but you know him, for he dwells with you and will be in you"* (Jn 14:16-17). He then elaborates, *"But the Helper, the Holy Spirit, whom the Father will send in my name, he will teach you all things, and bring to your remembrance all things that I said to you."* (14:26).

Jesus also said in this same passage, *"If anyone loves me, he will keep my word; and my Father will love him, and we will come to him and make our home with him"* (15:23). The Old Testament also agrees with this principle: *"But this is the Covenant that I will make with the house of Israel after those days," says the Lord. "I will put my law in their minds, and write it on their hearts; and I will be their God and they shall be my people"* (Jer 31:33).

Nevertheless, God is still interested in the Ten Commandments and in the stone tablets on which he wrote them. He showed me this one night after I lay awake listening to the reading of Genesis and Exodus on audio tapes.

To illustrate what I was hearing, the Lord sent into my spiritual vision a fragment of a stone tablet. The stone was smooth but not polished, light gray in color and had letters carved on it that I assumed were Hebrew. Then, to further reveal the carving, God showed me a close-up, as though he held up a magnifying glass to one of the Hebrew letters. I was amazed to see the deep groove of the Hebrew letter pock-marked with tiny random holes, as though a micro BB gun had shot the groove with tiny BBs.

The Bible says that God himself wrote on the stones: *Now the tablets were the work of God, and the writing was the writing of God on the tablets* (Ex 32:16). Could it be that the tiny fine lines of light I see at night, coming from the ceiling or the night sky, are the same type that made the BB markings? *God came from Teman, the Holy One from Mount Paran. His glory covered the heavens, and the earth was full of his praise. His brightness was like the light; he had rays flashing from his hand, and there his power was hidden* (Hab 3:3-4).

Not only do I see lines of light coming out of the sky toward me, I also discern the flickering of the Holy Spirit flame at special times of spiritual vision. Sometimes flames of the Holy Spirit encircle the heads of certain sanctified persons. A Methodist minister from Estonia who spoke at our church one night had wide bright flames around him.

I have just finished reading *A Divine Revelation of Hell* by Mary Baxter. The author tells in detail of Jesus taking her to hell in spirit every night for a period of 40 nights. She talked to the people who were standing in bowls of fire and being both burned and eaten by worms. Jesus asked her to tell people that hell is a real place. He also wants people to know how to stay out of there.

We have to repent of our sins, verbally acknowledge Jesus as Savior and Lord of our lives and believe that he was raised from the dead. Paul tells us in Romans: *If you confess with your mouth the Lord Jesus and believe in your heart that God has raised him from the dead, you will be saved. For with the heart one believes to righteousness, and with the mouth confession is made to salvation* (10:9-10).

This is the essential part of becoming a Christian, but the fruit of our conversion comes when we start living a righteous life, committed to doing daily what God wants us to do, loving everyone we meet, and praising him continually.

Scripture says flames are an essential passage on the way to both heaven and hell. Mark reports Christ's word: *"For everyone will be seasoned with fire ..."* (9:49). John the Baptist said, *"I baptize you with water unto repentance, but he who is coming after me is mightier than I, whose sandals I am not worthy to carry. He will baptize you with the Holy Spirit and fire"* (Mt 3:11).

Old Testament passages also speak of the cleansing and purifying that comes by fire. Malachi wrote, *"Behold, I send my messenger, and he will prepare the way before me .... But who can endure the day of his coming? And who can stand when he appears? For he is like a refiner's fire and like fullers' soap. ... For behold, the day is coming, burning like an oven, and all the proud, yes, all who do wickedly will be stubble. And the day which is coming shall burn them up," says the Lord of Hosts* (3:1-2; 4:1).

Isaiah, too, tells us that all have to pass through the flames. But just as Shadrack, Meshach and Abednigo were protected in the fiery furnace (Dan 3:8-30), those who know and fear the Lord will not be burned. *When you walk through the fire, you shall not be burned, nor shall the flame scorch you* (Isa 43:2). David wrote of God, *Who makes his angels spirits, his ministers a flame of fire* (Ps 104:4).

The third verse of that great old hymn "How Firm a Foundation" explains it all. "When through fiery trials thy pathway shall lie, my grace, all sufficient, shall be thy supply; the flame shall not hurt thee; I only design thy dross to consume, and thy gold to refine."

So what then is the difference in physical make-up between those going to heaven and those going to hell? Probably nothing. But heaven and hell are spiritual places. When one dies, the physical body decays. It is the spirit of a person, the complete essence of who the person is that remains intact.

God is the one who makes the decision as to whether the person's spirit is worth saving or throwing away, whether that spirit is to be further purified or burned up in flames that are as certain as death. The qualities that are godly will not burn. Everything else will.

One night when my publisher came to visit and prepare me to go to New York City to speak about my first book, *These Last Days,* the Lord wakened me at three in the morning and started filling the room with strange patterns of dark and light. They were angular, like many prisms packed together. It wasn't bright enough to be the Crystal Sea, I thought. I briefly wondered what was happening and wanted to be certain it was God, not evil. At that point, God knew my wondering and sent stacks of the brilliant jewels of heaven around the prisms. Then I heard a voice say, "Is the room prepared?" At that point, I slept and knew nothing more of what was going on or what the room was to be prepared for.

Miriam's daughter Deborah interpreted the vision thus: The prisms symbolized the Spirit river flowing out of the Throne of God, bringing his abundant grace to every situation. She quoted God as saying, "The river is still flowing, so why are you afraid?" This concept comes from Revelation: *And he showed me a pure river of water of life, clear as crystal, proceeding from the throne of God and of the Lamb* (22:1). So I need not fear any eventuality. I am being transformed into a person of spiritual and moral strength and integrity who can face these next months and years with equanimity.

There is a mysterious spiritual connection between people who love each other. I felt ill one Saturday evening, though nothing was actually wrong with me. Miriam and I attended the Childers Full Gospel Church Saturday night worship service, and as I sang, praised and prayed through a two-hour service, I totally recovered under the heavy anointing of the Holy Spirit. The next day I found out that my sister Betty was experiencing the beginnings of stomach flu, but it went away during the night. I think she received the healing of the Holy Spirit vicariously because of her closeness to me, while I was sitting under the strong anointing of God. There are many mysteries in the spiritual dimension that we cannot understand now.

In contrast to building a work by positive thoughts, we can lose a lot of blessings by being negative. Isaiah says of Jesus, *He was oppressed and he was afflicted, yet he opened not his mouth; he was led as a lamb to the slaughter, and as a sheep before its shearers is dumb, so he opened not his mouth* (53:7). If Jesus had complained of his fate and murmured against God, he could never have been the Savior of the world. He was simply silent.

There are many silences in this world: the silence of loneliness and rejection, of confrontation and conviction, of fear and judgment. The positive side of silence can be just as powerful. It can be a silence of love and forgiveness. Jesus showed this to the woman caught in adultery. It can be a silence of self-searching and contemplation, of meditation and listening prayer, of awe and profound worship of the holiness of God. God has graciously given the gift of silence to all of us at various times. I suggest that at least one day a week, we turn off the television and radio and become silent before our Maker.

A passage in Revelation mentions the silence before judgment: *When he opened the seventh seal, there was silence in heaven for about half an hour* (8:1). Before the Majestic Lord of the Universe, we are forced to wait in awesome silence. We are dust before him. Our frail and feeble struggles to tame our world crumble to nothing before his hurricanes, earthquakes and cosmic collisions. We even seek for ways to depict our universe artistically, but every art form we attempt miserably fails when compared with God's living model.

My father knew the value of silence because he loved to fish. He was never very good at catching them, but I like to think his simple act of holding a fishing pole in silence on the bank of a river allowed time for him to contemplate the wondrous God of the Universe and his own being in God's presence. Job 37:14 says: *"Stand still and consider the wondrous works of God."* David tells us in Psalm 46:10a: *Be still and know that I am God.*

Contemplating the silence of all humankind before God, I recall a poem I memorized more than 30 years ago. The title and author are presently unknown to me, but the poem as I remember it goes:

> I'll build me a silence of violets and clover,
> of voiceless blue Aprils and springs running over;
> of fawns lightly sleeping beneath the tall pines,
> nestling in vapors where star fire shines.
>
> I'll build me a silence where love is remembered,
> at the heart of a hill, cursed and cross-timbered;
> where God in his mercy absolves man of sins,
> where only God speaks and all silence begins.

12

Cosmic Cataclysm

It was nearly midnight at the Belle Starr Campground on Lake Eufala. This was the annual week-long summer encampment of Methodist families who had gathered to fellowship, laugh, eat camp food, play games and teach the children to water ski. The curtain of dust had settled, the windows were open and I lay in the camper listening to the gentle lapping of the waves against the lake shore. Then I became aware that something very special was about to happen.

Light from an unknown source bathed my body briefly before it withdrew to the ceiling where a message was presented in the form of an open-eyed vision. On the ceiling of the camper I saw the night sky with many stars. One of them exploded sending fragments spewing out in all directions. The vision ended with the stacks of prisms I am accustomed to seeing. I immediately asked God for the explanation of this vision. It was several weeks before an answer surfaced.

In the meantime, another message which arrived during that same camping trip was a call to prayer. I received a vision of a man praying. Actually I saw the side of his face with his hands in the prayer position. Prayer is the key to living life for God. Someone said prayer is the currency God uses. So I determined to spend more time in deep and fervent prayer.

Perhaps this was the impetus for Miriam and me to begin a weekly 24-hour bread-and-water fast. The object of the fast was to allow our spirits to get in touch with God's Spirit more easily. The first day I ate only dry bread and water instead of regular meals, yet I had so much energy I was able to do yard work all afternoon without tiring. While eating the bread, I remembered that more than half of the world's population have only bread and water to live on. The water in many nations is probably not all that pure either. The whole process was dedicated to the glory of God and in praise of the name Jesus.

On November 8, 1991, the Lord sent an amazing repeat vision of the exploding star vision I received in the summer. Planets were revolving around the sun. I knew they were our solar planets because Saturn's rings were visible. A small planet exploded and blew apart, flinging pieces in all directions. At the same time, the Lord said to me, "Mercury."

"Oh, great merciful heavens!" I thought. Is the Lord going to allow Mercury to explode, shifting the gravitational field of the entire universe, shaking all of the planets and changing their circuits around the sun? Besides that, where are the fragments of Mercury going to fall? Would the collision of great chunks of rocks with the earth generate the dust storm that darkens the sun and moon, causing most of the vegetation on earth to die? Matthew quotes Jesus saying, *"Immediately after the tribulation of those days the sun will be darkened, and the moon will not give its light; the stars will fall from heaven, and the powers of the heavens will be shaken"* (24:29).

The next day I proceeded to the library to research the planet Mercury in an encyclopedia. Mercury, it seems, is very hot and is the planet closest to the sun. It moves around the sun in 88 days, but the most interesting characteristic is its *very low gravity.* I also noticed that pictures of Mercury show great ridges around the surface which would be fracture points. Without sufficient gravity, it could disintegrate because of internal pressure.

So the planet Mercury is going to explode! That will be the catalyst for the awesome earthquakes, tidal waves, crumbling mountains and sinking islands, hurricanes, droughts and other catastrophes that will take place at the time of the tribulation.

> *I looked when he opened the sixth seal, and behold, there was a great earthquake, and the sun became black as sackcloth of hair, and the moon became like blood. And the stars of heaven fell to the earth, as a fig tree drops its late figs when it is shaken by a mighty wind.*
>
> *Then the sky receded as a scroll when it is rolled up, and every mountain and island was moved out of its place. And the kings of the earth, the great men, the rich men, the commanders, the mighty men, every slave and every free man, hid themselves in the caves and in the rocks of the mountains, and said to the mountains and rocks, "Fall on us and hide us from the face of him who sits on the throne and from the wrath of the Lamb! For the great day of his wrath has come, and who is able to stand?"* (Rev 6:12-17).

Also:

> *They shall go into the holes of the rocks, and into the caves of the earth, from the terror of the Lord and the glory of his majesty, when he arises to shake the earth mightily* (Isa 2:19).

Jesus said,

> *"And there will be signs in the sun, in the moon, and in the stars; and on the earth distress of nations, with perplexity, the sea*

and the waves roaring; men's hearts failing them from fear and the expectation of those things which are coming on the earth, for the powers of heaven will be shaken" (Lk 21:25-26).

On February 22, 1992, the Lord sent another confirmation of the cosmic explosion that is to occur and send the earth into a terrible tribulation. In a vision of the night sky, I saw huge rocks poised above the earth, debris from a space explosion, being readied to fall on the earth and cause massive destruction.

So destruction is to come from two different sources: atomic bombs carried by rockets, as mentioned above in chapter 6, and exploding planets and/or comets flinging debris all over the universe and shifting gravitational fields.

Two unrelated confirmations of these prophecies of the approaching destruction of America arrived at my doorstep. One came by way of a book, *Through the Fire Without Burning*, by Dumitri Duduman, a Romanian pastor who was sent by the Lord to the United States after the communist government of the Soviet Union collapsed. He was told by the Lord to warn the American people that vast destruction in the form of atomic bombs and fire will fall on certain large metropolises and that this destruction constitutes the judgment of the God of wrath upon this sinful nation.

The second confirmation was spoken by Anna, the director of the Lighthouse Outreach Rescue Mission, mentioned in an earlier chapter, who told the story of a minister delivering a revival message in Idaho a few years back. All at once, he interrupted the message with a prophecy from the Lord. He said, "The Lord is telling me that a time is coming soon when both coasts of the United States will be destroyed by fire, and people will flee to the middle of the country for safety."

Many times God has sent me visions of people fleeing from something. I have seen whole families hurriedly get into cars and drive away at high speed. I have seen people running away from something, and one woman turned and walked back alone. She was a young woman, wearing a blue jumper with a sad but resigned look on her face.

God sent a dream to reinforce the above conclusions. In the dream I was living in a small town when a warning of an approaching tornado was broadcast. We were instructed to drive west out of town, but most people were ignoring it. I thought I had several things to do before leaving. I had to find the key to a locker and deliver a package to a basement storage.

Arriving at the basement, I found it crowded with people who maintained they would be safe from the storm there. But I kept telling them we must go west, for that was the instruction. The basement would flood, I said. But nobody listened to me. They were laughing and partying and having a good time.

Because of the delay, the storm was almost upon me as I got into my car and headed west out of town. At the edge of town, a huge man as tall as a tree stepped to the middle of the street, stopped me and told me to come with him to a large brick and concrete building that was safe and secure from the storm. I knew it was an angel, so I went with him.

The first step up to the portico of the building was three or four feet high, and I had to struggle to climb up onto it. Arriving at the entrance to the building, I discovered the door would open only six or seven inches – no farther. "I can't get in here," I said to the angel.

"Yes, you can," he said. "Try harder." With super-human effort, I pushed through the opening and went in. I was immediately surrounded by smiling people who invited me to dinner. I was overwhelmed by the beauty of the room and the loving acceptance I felt. The atmosphere was warm and comforting, and I was home in heaven.

Somehow, I feel this is the way it is going to be at the end. All will have the opportunity to escape the wrath of God, but few will believe and accept it. The Way will be narrow and difficult, and many people will not want to expend the energy necessary to follow The Way because they won't think it is that important. Nor do they want to be ridiculed, laughed at or persecuted.

As Jesus said, *"Enter by the narrow gate; for wide is the gate and broad is the way that leads to destruction, and there are many who go in by it. Because narrow is the gate and confined is the way which leads to life, and there are few who find it"* (Mt 7:13-14). And then, *"So the last will be first, and the first last. For many are called but few chosen"* (Mt 20:16).

13

The Land

The Lord called me to Israel last October. An opportunity came to visit the Holy Land during the Feast of Tabernacles celebration, and I felt the Lord urging me to go. After I arrived there, I found out why. The Spirit of God was so powerful in the land of Israel, particularly in Jerusalem, that one can sense a holiness encompassing everything. God took the occasion of my being in this sacred place to reveal additional prophecies concerning the end times.

Even the plane trip was exciting to me. I had never crossed the Atlantic Ocean before, so it was with considerable delight that I experienced being 30,000 feet over the ocean to Paris, Rome, the Mediterranean Sea, the Island of Cyprus and finally, Tel Aviv, Israel.

As we landed at the Tel Aviv airport, I noticed mature cotton plants ready to harvest on either side of the paved runway. I thought, how efficient the Israelis are to use every available space for planting. In this way many fruits and vegetables are grown in Israel, watered by deep wells and the Jordan River. How I would soon enjoy these fresh fruits and vegetables! This Holy Land really seems to be the land of plenty.

Since I am a bird-watcher, I always have an eye out for unfamiliar species. While still at the airport, I saw pigeons and the ubiquitous house sparrows. Binoculars would have helped, but I did make out a small wren that closely resembled our Carolina wren; also gray-backed crows and a white egret at the Sea of Galilee. Later, while visiting the Masada, I saw small pipits, also blackbirds with white wing linings. Huge ravens, like the ones that fed Elijah, glided over bare desert near the Dead Sea.

We arrived at the hotel in Tiberias after dark, so the first thing I did after waking in the morning was to rush outside to see the Sea of Galilee. I cried as I stood by that beautiful clear lake, realizing that Jesus had spent most of his life here. The beach was covered with pebbles, not sand, and I could visualize fishing nets stretched out on it to dry.

I could also imagine Jesus and his disciples in the midst of crowds of people gathered near the shore. I walked to the edge and tested the temperature of the water with my fingers. It did not feel cold on that early October day; a mid-western American could swim in it with comfort.

I did not swim in the Sea of Galilee, but I was baptized in the Jordan River, which feeds the Sea. Though I had been baptized previously, I could not pass up an opportunity for a rededication of my baptismal vows at the spot on earth where many feel John the Baptizer baptized Jesus.

The lesson I learned during that service was unforgettable and if I had decided to abstain from this re-baptismal rite, I would have missed it. We were gathered on bleachers beside the river and had begun our worship service to prepare for the baptism when the leader of another group interrupted us and said her group was scheduled to use the facility at that time. The tone of her voice was strident and clashed with the tender atmosphere of the moment.

Faylene, our leader, responded to her with a smile, "As you can see, we have already begun our service, so why don't you join us?"

"No," the other leader replied. "We want to conduct our own service."

At that, Faylene smiled, and with a gentle voice said, "All right." She turned to us and said with a soft voice and a smile, "Folks, we are going to pause and allow another group to go ahead of us." Then she sat down.

As long as I live, I will never forget the lesson Faylene taught us that day by being kind to someone who had been rude.

The ancient city of Capernaum, situated on the north shore of the Sea of Galilee, consists of ruins of what was once a beautiful synagogue and the stone wall remains of village houses. One of those houses belonged to the Apostle Peter, whom Jesus visited many times. Along these shores are located Roman Catholic churches, built over sites estimated to be places where Jesus performed miracles of feeding the 5,000 and preaching the Sermon on the Mount. All of these places were very special to me. When I close my eyes, I can still see all of them and feel close to the Living Christ.

The Golan Heights occupy the east side of Galilee. From the top of those hills, we could see all of the Sea of Galilee and much of the fertile Jordan Valley. It was easy to understand the military importance of the Golan Heights.

After visiting the modern city of Nazareth, we set out by bus for Jerusalem. What wonderful worship services we held on the bus every morning as we started touring. Any pain, uneasy stomach, sore throat or headache disappeared after 15 minutes of singing God's praises and praying for his presence with us. I couldn't have asked for a kinder or more congenial group of people with whom to travel.

We spent the daylight hours in Jerusalem visiting the Garden of Gethsemane, the Garden Tomb and the old walled city which encloses the Western Wall. We were told that the Wailing Wall is not a wall of the old temple, restored by Zerubbabel during the first return of the captives from Babylon, but the remains of a retaining wall adjacent to the old temple.

Jesus' prophecy of the temple destruction was fulfilled in A.D. 70 by the Romans: *Then, as some spoke of the temple, how it was adorned with beautiful stones and donations, [Jesus] said, "As for these things which you see, the days will come in which not one stone shall be left upon another that shall not be thrown down"* (Lk 21:5-6).

Evenings were special because we participated in the Christian commemoration of the Feast of Tabernacles celebration as described in Zechariah: *And it shall come to pass that everyone who is left of all the nations which came against Jerusalem shall go up from year to year to worship the King, the Lord of hosts, and to keep the Feast of Tabernacles* (14:16).

We met Christian people from 80 nations, 4,000 in all, some of whom traveled half-way around the world to attend this festival. Christians are grafted in, according to St. Paul, for Abraham is our father too, by faith, not by blood (Rom 11).

An orchestra composed of musicians from many nations accompanied a choir as singing, dancing and speeches filled every evening. Specially made fringed banners trimmed in silver and gold, red and purple, or yellow and green satin were carried down the aisles or hung in various locations. The beauty of the banners was breathtaking; sparkling colors held by beautiful people. My chest burned like a glowing coal of fire when the entire roomful of people stood and sang, "Alleluia."

At the end of the first evening, people of all nations were weeping for joy, hugging and shaking hands with each other in the aisles and hallways. One big smiling Brazilian man grabbed me and kissed me on both cheeks, while repeating "Shalom."

That very night the Lord wakened me with a vision of a huge heavenly choir singing "Sound the Trumpet in Zion." Then I saw single faces float by. I had a feeling they were members of the heavenly choir, and I should know some of them. Perhaps they had changed in appearance since I last saw them. After thinking about it for a while, I decided the heavenly choir was singing with the people from all over the world who had come to Jerusalem for the Feast of Tabernacles celebration.

The next morning, the big parade day, the Lord wakened me, showing me a heavenly parade. The marchers were in glorious heavenly dress: gold, red, white and sparkling silver, violet and blue. Row after row of them, marching ten or twelve abreast, paraded by in precise rows and perfect step. I lay watching this perfection cross my spirit vision while joy flooded my heart.

The terrestrial parade was not quite so perfect, but the same joy was present. We marched through the streets of Jerusalem holding banners, all 4,000 of us, while giving small flags and candy to the children in the streets and shouting "shalom" or "we love you" to the quarter-of-a-million spectators. They, in turn, responded in like fashion. The Holy Spirit was powerfully present for I marched for three hours, dancing part of the time, and still had energy to walk another mile back to the hotel. God is so good, and he loves Jerusalem.

The old walled city of Jerusalem comprises only a small part of the metropolis of Jerusalem. The impression I received from our hotel's eighth floor window was of whiteness and cleanliness–indeed, a beautiful city of a 400,000 population. Buildings are primarily of concrete because lumber is scarce and expensive. Even in the Biblical days of David and Solomon, lumber for building was brought in from Lebanon (1 Kings 5:6). Few trees remain in Jerusalem proper, and they are small. Olive trees abound, even on dry hills, for they require little water.

We also visited several places of interest in greater Jerusalem. The tour to the Holocaust Museum, the Yad Vashem Sanctuary on Remembrance Mount, was a deeply emotional experience. Rooms of pictures captured the history of the Nazi persecution of the Jews, culminating in large photographs of the death camps where millions of Jews and non-Jews were gassed and burned.

The most emotionally moving part of the museum was the Children's Hall where the light of six small candles reflected by a thousand mirrors glowed as stars on the ceiling of the darkened room. At the same time the names, ages and nationalities of all of the children who died in the holocaust were spoken one by one. We could not keep the tears back as we struggled to comprehend the enormity of the tragedy. One of the women in our group sobbed uncontrollably as she sensed within her spirit the grief of the parents and relatives of these children.

The resolution of this catastrophe can only come at the close of the age when all people are judged. Yes, thank God, it will be resolved. However, there is still time for a repentance of those sins and a restoration of the sinners. I know I have asked God for forgiveness of my sins and have been forgiven.

Also to be resolved on that day will be the judgment of unrepentant nations and peoples who are participating in the slaughter of unborn children. Who can know what gifts these children might have brought to the world: a cure for cancer, a peace plan which works, a musical or artistic masterpiece, a conservation program which could save the earth, a special insight into the mind and plan of God himself, or perhaps a new concept on how to love unlovely people. But their existence doesn't even have to be justified. Mine wasn't.

Another day we stopped at the National Museum of Israel where replicas of the Dead Sea Scrolls are exhibited. We saw copies of Old Testament Scriptures thousands of years old. The complete manuscript of the book of Isaiah has been found, and it authenticates the literal translations that have come to us from other historic sources.

A sense of holiness and awe pervaded the museum. Perhaps the abstract sculptures situated around the grounds reflected the constraint of the Second Commandment, *"You shall not make for yourself any carved image, or any likeness of anything that is in heaven above, or that is in the earth beneath, or that is in the waters under the earth; you shall not bow down to them nor serve them ..."* (Deut 5:8-9). Though these sculptures represented nothing alive, they did capture my attention and challenged my imagination.

One day we rode the bus to the Dead Sea. It was downhill all the way, from an altitude of about 4,000 feet above sea level at Jerusalem to 1,200 feet *below* sea level at the Dead Sea. The sea was clear; we could see the bottom. But it felt oily because of the 25 percent salts it contains. I did not swim in it because those with high blood pressure were warned not to expose themselves to the salt. The guide said we could explode after ten minutes in that salty water.

The sea is shrinking at the rate of about one vertical foot per year because Jordan River water that feeds it is being used almost entirely for irrigation; also the sea itself is being pumped out and evaporated for harvesting salts.

A fabulous resort hotel graced the beach. Many people

come to this balmy winter resort to expose their bodies to the Dead Sea salts as a cure for skin problems. The heavy air was a little oppressive to me, but I appreciated the view, the desert warmth and the constant sunshine.

The Masada is awesome. Glaring sun beats down on that small plateau all the time. It measures 300 by 650 meters and rises about 1,200 ft. above the Dead Sea. We could see the entire south half of the Dead Sea from the top. The Masada is bare of vegetation except for one small juniper-like tree. I understood why Jonah needed shade in this desert, but we were there early enough in the morning to avoid mid-day heat.

Earlier one of the Herod kings of Israel had built up this plateau as a fortress, including a stone palace for himself and reservoirs to hold stored water. We saw one cistern that held 40,000 cubic meters of water, enough it is estimated to furnish water for 5,000 people for ten years. A Roman general named Flavius Silva took three years to build a ramp up to the top and seized the plateau from the Jewish Zealots who were secluded there. But it was too late; the Zealots had already killed themselves. This happened around A.D. 70.

Another morning we rode the tour bus to Bethlehem to visit the birthplace of Jesus, a small cave now covered by both a Roman Catholic and an adjoining Eastern Orthodox Church. Worship services were being celebrated in both churches, but the cave was at a lower level and we could see it without interrupting the services.

Most nights the Lord was powerfully present in the hotel room. My roommate and I did not interrupt the holiness in that room by turning on television. We just enjoyed talking over the day, writing in our journals, and reading our Bibles.

Spectacular visions came to me at night while I was in Jerusalem. One night I wakened looking at the wall, when it became a screen. The entire wall glowed and flickered with white and golden light as God prepared to give me a message. The first picture I saw in the middle of the flickering screen was the tortured face of Jesus. Then appeared the normal face of Jesus. It looked like the portrait of Jesus which is displayed on the book cover of my first book, *These Last Days.* I knew that this meant the vision was originating with Jesus.

After that I saw bare dirt. The vision showed movement of land as though I were in a helicopter flying over desert land. Miles and miles of lifeless earth passed under my vision. It did not resemble a normal sandy desert, but looked rather like dried-up pasture land and brown, desolate fields. After that I saw American flags, which meant the dry earth was America. In the midst of the barren earth lay bare bones.

The vision then switched to scenes of blue United Nations helmets, then U.S. khaki helmets. After that I saw an upside-down cross, which I interpreted to mean betrayal. Then I recognized an unmistakable Chinese coolie hat, like an inverted cone, followed by fire, much fire, covering the entire screen.

The visions seemed to be over, so I immediately grabbed my notebook, crept to the bathroom to avoid waking my roommate and wrote what I had just seen. I continued to sit in the bathroom, shaking with the wonder of it all. I prayed for wisdom to interpret the visions, then returned to bed.

No sooner had I become settled and relaxed when the visions started again, this time on the opposite wall. The first thing I saw was an oriental face with a stringy mustache and a small, thin goatee. That disappeared, and I saw lines of light shooting out of a central point, flying in all directions. From previous experience, I knew this meant atomic missiles. Then I saw American flags again. The flags faded, then came the fire, a long period of brilliant flames covering the entire wall screen. At that, the visions ceased, and I was left to interpret them.

Though I didn't sleep much the remainder of the night, morning found me alert enough to reflect on what I had seen the night before. I believe God was telling me the United States is going to be betrayed and bombed either by China or another oriental nation.

Isaiah tells of God calling birds of prey from the east to punish the sinful city of Babylon, which could also symbolize America in the late 20th century. *"I am God, and there is none like me, declaring the end from the beginning, and from ancient times things that are not yet done, saying 'My counsel shall stand, and I will do all my pleasure,' calling a bird of prey from the east, the man who executes my counsel, from a far country. Indeed I have spoken it; I will also bring it to pass, I have purposed it; I will also do it"* (46:9-11). God punctuated this Scripture by showing me a vision of our beautiful sapphire planet rolling down the wall and disappearing.

Either before or after that, a terrible drought will sweep across the nation during which many people will die of hunger and thirst. As of the beginning of 1996, a severe drought is already occurring in Angola and Mozambique, Africa, where the croplands lie bare from lack of rain even in the rainy season; the trees are dying, the rivers are running dry and thousands of people have no food or water.

Another possible explanation of the vision of dry earth is a drought of spirit. Amos, who lived around 755 B.C., talks about this: *"Behold, the days are coming,"* says the Lord God, *"that I will send a famine on the land, not a famine for bread, nor a thirst for water, but of hearing the words of the Lord .... They shall run to and fro, seeking the word of the Lord, but shall not find it"* (8:11-12).

Whether of famine, atomic bombs, cosmic catastrophes or simply the absence of the Holy Spirit, a time is coming soon when vast destruction is going to occur across the face of the planet. Those who are ready for the return of Jesus will be taken out of danger and into glory where they will be safe and happy forever.

The most inspirational day for me of the visit to Israel was the last holy place we visited—the Garden Tomb. After passing through a narrow street, we entered the gate of a walled enclosure. It was as though we had entered Eden—a beautiful garden of flowers, flowering trees and singing birds of several different varieties. It seemed more like spring than fall. Walkways with garden benches connected all parts of the garden to the tomb area. The tomb itself had been discovered by excavation and was 25 feet lower than the surrounding garden.

The cave tomb showed evidence of having been chipped out of rock and must have taken much time and money. There was space for two or three people to be laid out flat, but of course it was empty. I did not feel a special nearness to God inside the tomb, but while we were sitting on benches in the middle of that sacred garden waiting for everyone to see it, a powerful sense of peace and serenity enveloped me. I knew without question that this was where Jesus had risen from the dead.

This was where our faith began, and this is where Jesus will return and establish his kingdom on earth. The land that is very far off will become the headquarters and center of God's kingdom forever.

14

The Rapture

Shortly after Howard died, at the urging of Miriam, I traveled with church friends to Carthage, Missouri, to visit the "Precious Moments" park and museum. Still being in a daze from the grief, I wandered around the museum by myself most of the morning. The artistry of the museum was impressive, but I wasn't seeing it.

At lunch time, I circled the dining room looking for an empty table, but there were none. Just then, a woman at one table invited me to join her and her husband. Their smiling eyes gleamed with hospitality, and I accepted their invitation with silent thanks to God. This couple appeared to be about retirement age but looked healthy and active. They told me they were traveling evangelists and were about ready to retire.

As we shared a table blessing together and ate our sandwiches, the woman, Ruby Benning, looked at me intently as though trying to see inside. Satisfied that I would receive her offering, she told a story with such a powerful impact I still shake in awe when I think about it.

Ruby had been a devoted Christian for many years, but was afflicted with a severe form of arthritis, which prevented her from traveling with her husband Robert in his ministry. She had faithfully stayed home, praying fervently and continually for him and his work and for her healing so she could help him. Years passed, and there was no change in her condition, though she firmly believed in faith healing. It simply wasn't happening to her.

In the early morning hours of one particular day, Ruby was not sleeping well because of the pain, so she rose from bed and went to stand by the window in the living room. She started to pray. When she next looked out the window, she noticed a glow high in the sky. She opened her mouth in amazement as the glow brightened and changed color from yellow to pink to violet, then silvery white.

A figure began to emerge from the center of this glow, and she observed with wonder and great joy that the figure was Jesus! The whole sky brightened with his glory, and the panorama slowly started descending toward the ground. As it did so, she heard music from a heavenly choir. Then, remembering her husband, she screamed, "It's the Rapture! Bob, get up! *Jesus is coming,* and it's the Rapture!"

Ruby's heart pounded within her as she continued to watch the figure of Jesus descend from the sky closer and closer toward her own yard. The glorious light continued to glow around him, and the music reached crescendo proportions. Jesus drifted down behind some trees where she couldn't see him, but the glow was still in the trees, and she knew he was there. *"Bob!"* she yelled again with even more emphasis. *"Jesus is here, and it's the Rapture! Get up!"* But her husband did not emerge from the bedroom.

An inner voice told Ruby to open the door and greet Jesus, so she rushed to the front door and threw it open. There, on her doorstep, appeared the One she had worshipped and loved since she was a child. He stood at her front door, surrounded by all his glory. Jesus didn't exactly walk; rather he swept into the house and over to her, first looking intently into her eyes, then touching her on the shoulder. He had the most beautiful, loving face she had ever seen and he was smiling, she said.

At that moment her husband Bob, with his hand on her shoulder, shook her awake and said, "Ruby – Ruby, you've been having a bad dream and screaming."

As she slowly wakened and moved, Ruby realized that the pain and swelling in her joints was completely gone. She had been totally healed. From then on, Ruby traveled with her husband, telling the story of her miracle and teaching Bible stories to children while her husband, Evangelist Bob, preached the Gospel of Jesus Christ to their parents.

This scenario could well be the way it happens when Jesus does come for his saints in the Church Universal. But instead of waking up in bed, we will awake in heaven.

One morning late in 1995, I started to get up, but the Lord said, "Stay put." I lay back down and reached a state of complete relaxation when the Lord said, "A week – by the year 2,000." At the same time I felt the electric shock of the Holy Spirit traveling throughout my body. Immediately I thought of the end times the Lord has been warning me about. My mind started searching for an interpretation of this prophecy.

Peter explains how God thinks about time: *"Beloved, do not forget this one thing, that with the Lord one day is as a thousand years, and a thousand years as one day"* (2 Pet 3:8). This concept comes from Moses: *"For a thousand years in your sight are like yesterday when it is past, and like a watch in the night"* (Ps 90:4).

At first I thought the Lord meant he would come within a week of the year 2,000. But that didn't fit the message. So I started remembering the book of Daniel where the phrase "70 weeks" meant 70 weeks of years. Sixty-nine of those weeks of years, or 483 years, was given as the time the order was put out for the children of Israel to return to Jerusalem after the Babylonian captivity until the coming of the Messiah (Dan 9:24-25). This prophecy was fulfilled when Jesus was born.

In the same manner, the Lord's prophecy of a week by the year 2,000 could mean seven *thousand* years of humankind on earth will be completed by the year 2,000. Seven is the Biblical perfect number.

This prophecy, coupled with the statement from the Lord in my book, *These Last Days,* that this is *the last decade,* could mean humanity will have experienced 7,000 years of life on earth by then, and after that God will call into effect the end-time events. These are described symbolically in the book of Revelation and in the words of Jesus in the Gospels. Also Romans tells us: *For [God] will finish the work and cut it short in righteousness, because the Lord will make a short work upon the earth* (9:28).

(This short work could refer to the time human beings, descendants of Adam, are given to live on this planet. It is not to infer how long the earth has existed. God's days in the book of Genesis could extend hundreds of millions of years to us mortals.)

I believe this means the Rapture will take place sometime in or near the year 2,000. God will call up the Church Universal with its millions of saints to meet Jesus in the air, and we will be with him forever.

Since the Holy Spirit was sent as a gift to the church, it is logical for God to withdraw the Holy Spirit from the earth along with the Church. This will allow Satan to inflict his worst on the planet and on those people who remain. Paul suggests this truth: *And now you know what is restraining, that he may be revealed in his own time. For the mystery of lawlessness is already at work; only he who now restrains will do so until he is taken out of the way* (2 Thess 2:6-7).

I interpret the identity of the One who restrains to be the Holy Spirit. At that time, the earth is likely to become a place of utmost horror: violence, starvation, disease, insanity and cataclysmic disasters that strip people of the least fragment of human dignity. Therefore, it is terribly important for us to bring into the kingdom all of our friends, relatives, neighbors and acquaintances – everyone within the reach of our persuasion.

Paul told Timothy in his first letter, *"Preach the word! Be ready in season and out of season. Convince, rebuke, exhort, with all long-suffering and teaching"* (4:2). Those who receive the call and feel God's hand on them to be missionaries will take the Gospel of Jesus Christ to the whole world according to Matthew 28:19.

I am aware that Jesus himself said, in referring to his return, *"But of that day and hour no one knows, no, not even the angels of heaven, but my Father only"* (Mt 24:36). We cannot know the day or hour of Christ's return, but we can and should know the *season* of his return because Jesus said we could.

After Jesus explained to his disciples the events of the coming "Day of the Lord," they questioned him further: *And they answered and said to him, "Where, Lord?" So he said to them, "Wherever the body is, there the eagles will be gathered together"* (Lk 17:37).

Certainly, in my opinion, because of the moral atmosphere of this nation and of the whole world, the stench of evil everywhere, it is evident that the body is on the ground, and the eagles are gathering. It should follow, therefore, that the season is approaching and the Lord is preparing to come for his saints.

There are at least two passages in the Bible that tell us God will guide us into the future with prior warnings. One is in Isaiah where God is speaking, *"Behold, the former things have come to pass, and new things I declare; before they spring forth, I tell you of them"* (42:9). The second is recorded in John's gospel where Jesus is speaking, *"However, when he, the Spirit of truth, has come, he will guide you into all truth, for he will not speak on his own authority, but whatever he hears he will speak, and he will tell you things to come"* (16:13).

For those who are left after the Rapture, a terrible tribulation is to occur on the earth: atomic war over the whole world; drought and famine; rampant, incurable diseases and pestilences; earthquakes; hurricanes; tidal waves; wild fires and vast destruction from an exploding planet and/or comets, raining down huge rocks on the earth. We are seeing the beginnings or foothills of the tribulation even now, in the middle of 1990s.

Those called up to be with the Lord will be safe from this destruction. As Paul wrote to the church at Thessalonica: *For the Lord himself will descend from heaven with a shout, with the voice of an archangel, and with the trumpet of God. And the dead in Christ will rise first. Then we who are alive and remain shall be caught up together with them in the clouds to meet the Lord in the air. And thus we shall always be with the Lord. Therefore comfort one another with these words (*1 Thess 4:16-18).

Jesus gave this message about the end times: *"Then the sign of the Son of Man will appear in heaven, and then all the tribes of the earth will mourn, and they will see the Son of Man coming on the clouds of heaven with power and great glory. And he will send his angels with a great sound of a trumpet, and they will gather together his elect from the four winds, from one end of heaven to the other"* (Mt 24:30-31).

The elect are those who have declared their faith in Jesus, have accepted his forgiveness and have lived their lives following his example. They are destined to live with him in glory forever.

An anointed young prophet laid hands on me one evening when the Holy Spirit was powerfully present in a worship service and said I was ordained to live long enough to hear the trumpets of God announce the close of the age. Praise God!

I experienced a small taste of heaven not long ago. I was working on the computer, composing this book, and it seemed as if the Lord himself were giving me every word. I finished with the morning's work and stepped into the kitchen to fix a sandwich, when a wave of glory hit me. I felt a flood of joy touch my entire being.

The word "love" kept coming to me, and I realized I was so in love with everybody in the world that my head and whole body were about to burst with joy of the purest kind. I danced around the kitchen to the music in my heart and my eyes filled with tears of joy. "Can heaven be any better than this?" I thought. But this joy was only temporary. Heavenly love and joy and peace will be forever!

Dottie Mae Goard lives in Oklahoma where she is a certified Lay Speaker for the United Methodist Church. An accomplished poet, she devotes time to her writing, an active life of prayer, birdwatching and being a volunteer in nonprofit, church-related projects.

Additional copies of this book may be obtained
from your local bookstore,
or by sending $14.95 per copy, postpaid,

to:

Hope Publishing House
P.O. Box 60008
Pasadena, CA 91116

CA residents please add 8¼% sales tax
FAX orders to: (626) 792-2121
Telephone VISA/MC orders to (800) 326-2671
E-mail orders to: hopepub@loop.com
Visit our Web site: http://www.hope-pub.com